[H.A.S.C. No. 115–28]

THREATS TO SPACE ASSETS AND IMPLICATIONS FOR HOMELAND SECURITY

JOINT HEARING

BEFORE THE

SUBCOMMITTEE ON STRATEGIC FORCES

OF THE

COMMITTEE ON ARMED SERVICES

MEETING JOINTLY WITH

SUBCOMMITTEE ON EMERGENCY PREPAREDNESS, RESPONSE, AND COMMUNICATIONS

OF THE

COMMITTEE ON HOMELAND SECURITY

[Serial No. 115–12]

HOUSE OF REPRESENTATIVES

ONE HUNDRED FIFTEENTH CONGRESS

FIRST SESSION

HEARING HELD
MARCH 29, 2017

U.S. GOVERNMENT PUBLISHING OFFICE

25–094

WASHINGTON : 2017

CONTENTS

Page

STATEMENTS PRESENTED BY MEMBERS OF CONGRESS

WITNESSES

APPENDIX

THREATS TO SPACE ASSETS AND IMPLICATIONS FOR HOMELAND SECURITY

House of Representatives, Committee on Armed Services, Subcommittee on Strategic Forces, Meeting Jointly with the Committee on Homeland Security, Subcommittee on Emergency Preparedness, Response, and Communications, *Washington, DC, Wednesday, March 29, 2017.*

The subcommittees met, pursuant to call, at 2:02 p.m., in Room HVC–210, Capitol Visitor Center, Hon. Mike Rogers (chairman of the Strategic Forces Subcommittee) presiding.

OPENING STATEMENT OF HON. MIKE ROGERS, A REPRESENTATIVE FROM ALABAMA, CHAIRMAN, SUBCOMMITTEE ON STRATEGIC FORCES, COMMITTEE ON ARMED SERVICES

Mr. Rogers. Good afternoon. I want to welcome you to this hearing on "Threats to Space Assets and Implications for Homeland Security," held jointly by the House Armed Services Subcommittee on Strategic Forces and the Homeland Security Subcommittee on Emergency Preparedness, Response, and Communications.

I want to start by thanking our witnesses for being here and taking the time to prepare. I know it takes a lot of time to prepare for these and make your expertise available. We have an expert panel with us regarding topics of space and homeland security. Though testifying in their personal capacities, they each have decades worth of experience with the issues being discussed here today.

Our witnesses are General William Shelton, retired Air Force and former commander of U.S. Air Force Space Command; Admiral Thad Allen, retired Coast Guard and member of the GPS Advisory Board and former commandant of the U.S. Coast Guard; and the Honorable Joseph Nimmich, former deputy administrator, Federal Emergency Management Agency and retired rear admiral, U.S. Coast Guard.

I also want to thank Chairman Donovan and Ranking Member Payne for joining us in support of this hearing. We have heard extensively from Department of Defense and intelligence community officials regarding the potential foreign threats to our space systems. The threats are real, serious, and only getting worse.

Unfortunately, talking about a conflict extending to space isn't science fiction anymore and the impact of that threat extends beyond the military. It extends to our way of life here in the United States. There likely isn't a person in this hearing room, nor within the entire Capitol campus that hasn't utilized the services provided by satellites at some point today.

For instance, aside from DIRECTV and DISH satellite TV, which allow me to watch Alabama play football on Saturdays no matter where I am—Roll Tide—the Global Positioning System, or GPS, is probably the most widely known space asset and for good reason. While I think many recognize that GPS powers their navigation in their cars and cellphones, they may not know or may not recognize the support it provides to financial transactions, farming, shipping, public safety, environmental monitoring, and a host of other areas.

The American public may also not realize that GPS is built and operated [by] the United States Air Force. Potential adversaries recognize our dependence on it. I guarantee you that.

And GPS is one of many important space systems. We spend time in the Armed Services Committee understanding what the loss of space would mean to the military and that we need to protect and defend those assets. But what does a loss of space mean to our economy and our financial institutions, our agricultural activities, our transportation and infrastructure?

Today our witnesses will help us understand the importance and role of space regarding our homeland security and our emergency preparedness. The public deserves to know what is at stake when we are talking about the risk of loss to our access to space. It is my sincere hope that a conflict never reaches into space, but conflict has extended across air, land and sea, and cyberspace. Hearings like this are needed to make sure we are aware of the consequences we now face if it ever does happen and ensure that we are ready for it.

I will now turn to Chairman Donovan for any opening statement he may have and then to Mr. Garamendi today, standing in for Ranking Member Cooper, and Mr. Payne after that.

So Chairman Donovan is recognized.

[The prepared statement of Mr. Rogers can be found in the Appendix on page 27.]

OPENING STATEMENT OF HON. DANIEL M. DONOVAN, JR., A REPRESENTATIVE FROM NEW YORK, CHAIRMAN, SUBCOMMITTEE ON EMERGENCY PREPAREDNESS, RESPONSE, AND COMMUNICATIONS, COMMITTEE ON HOMELAND SECURITY

Mr. DONOVAN. Thank you, Mr. Chairman.

And thank you to all of our witnesses.

I would like to thank you, Chairman, for holding this hearing today and including my subcommittee in this very important and timely discussion.

In today's world, our lives are connected more than ever before and this is because of our space-based capabilities, specifically satellites. Without satellites, we cannot make financial transactions, communicate with cellphones, navigate from one location to another, fly airplanes, watch television, or effectively prepare for and respond to natural disasters or, God forbid, terrorist attacks.

Space-based capabilities, like global positioning systems, satellite communications, and remote sensing, not only help our military operations, but have made it safer for our first responders to effectively and efficiently respond to a crisis or emergency.

Nearly 5 years ago, my district, which includes Staten Island and parts of Brooklyn, was devastated by Superstorm Sandy. This perfect storm caused dozens of New Yorkers to lose their lives, thousands of homes destroyed or damaged, and for millions of dollars being used and spent on reconstructing communities, including my own.

The preparedness and response efforts directed at Superstorm Sandy, while not perfect, were much better than previous major disasters, like Hurricane Katrina. Satellite capabilities were part of the reason first responders and government agencies had the information needed to respond decisively and quickly.

Satellites are being used to enhance our Nation's preparedness and response efforts, especially when critical infrastructure is damaged, destroyed, or overloaded. I saw this firsthand during Superstorm Sandy. Prior to Superstorm Sandy making landfall, the Federal Emergency Management Agency [FEMA] used the storm tracking predictions from weather satellites to pre-position equipment and resources all along the east coast. Additionally, FEMA used satellite imagery to expedite the disaster declaration process and provide assistance to impacted areas.

During this response effort, teams deployed satellite communications equipment and high-throughput satellite terminals to provide voice and internet connectivity to first responders and survivors. These are a few of the growing reasons why satellite capabilities are key to our homeland security.

While we need to continue to look for ways to incorporate space-based capabilities into our preparedness and response efforts, we need to be cognizant of the threat to those space systems. There are numerous threats, whether intentional or naturally occurring, that could damage or destroy our satellites and significantly reduce the lifesaving capabilities they provide for our first responders. I am particularly interested in learning more today about how our Nation's preparedness and response efforts could be impacted if our space capabilities were diminished.

I want to thank our distinguished panel again for testifying this afternoon, and I look forward to learning more about what we in Congress can do to help ensure our Nation's military and first responders don't lose these vital capabilities.

Mr. Chairman, I yield back the remainder of my time.

[The prepared statement of Mr. Donovan can be found in the Appendix on page 29.]

Mr. ROGERS. The Chair now recognizes Mr. Garamendi for 5 minutes.

STATEMENT OF HON. JOHN GARAMENDI, A REPRESENTATIVE FROM CALIFORNIA, SUBCOMMITTEE ON STRATEGIC FORCES, COMMITTEE ON ARMED SERVICES

Mr. GARAMENDI. Thank you very much, Mr. Chairman and Chairman Donovan. Thank you for doing the joint hearing. I think it is extremely important.

I know that our chairman has spent a great deal of time bringing us information on communication systems and the vulnerabilities as well as the potential that they have, both, mostly in the military area, but also as it extends beyond that.

We do know there is enormous vulnerability on the military side, as the chairman pointed out. We have also spent some time looking at the domestic vulnerability, mostly as it has occurred on another subcommittee on which I am on, which is the Coast Guard and

Maritime. And the Coast Guard has had in the past the navigational portfolio of the Federal Government.

So we have looked at this and now bringing together these issues is extremely important and to look at the continental United States, Alaska, and Hawaii and other areas in the context of satellite communication and the necessity for a backup system or how to deal with all the benefits that those satellite communication systems bring to us from GPS and beyond is extremely important.

I thank you for doing this. Mr. Cooper was called away to a meeting, and I was the only option available at the time he left, so he put me in this position.

[Laughter.]

Thank you very much.

Mr. ROGERS. Thank you. And Mr. Payne's statement will be taken for the record when he arrives.

So we will turn to our witness panel, and we will start with General Shelton. And, General Shelton, before you start, I understand you have got some guests with you today.

General SHELTON. Actually, I do. I have got my daughter and her husband and my two grandsons.

Mr. ROGERS. Welcome to the hearing. Your granddaddy's an American hero. All right.

General SHELTON. Thank you, sir.

Mr. ROGERS. The floor is yours.

STATEMENT OF GEN WILLIAM L. SHELTON, USAF (RET.), FORMER COMMANDER, U.S. AIR FORCE SPACE COMMAND

General SHELTON. Chairman Rogers, Chairman Donovan, and Mr. Garamendi and distinguished members of the committees, thank you for your invitation to appear today to discuss threats to our space assets and the implication of those threats to our homeland security.

I believe the vast majority of our American citizens are not conscious of these threats and are therefore blissfully unaware of the impacts on our way of life should conflict extend to space. I commend your committees for taking up this subject.

There is a host of satellites that provide services essential to modern life in the United States and across the planet. In fact, according to the latest edition of the Space Report published annually by the Space Foundation, the global space industry is a $325 billion enterprise.

Satellite-provided services have become analogous to electricity, a utility we really take for granted. Most of us don't need to, nor want to, know where or how our power is produced, but we expect our local power company to continuously provide the power we need to heat and cool our houses and run our myriad electrical devices. Space services are now a utility as well. Few Americans understand that fact.

In contrast, potential adversaries are well aware of our dependence on satellites. Continuous combat operations since Operation Desert Storm in 1991 have provided an unparalleled learning laboratory for them. Not surprisingly, nations are now actively testing methods to deny us continued use of space services during conflict.

They have developed a full quiver of these methods, ranging from satellite signal jamming to outright destruction of satellites via a kill vehicle, such as successfully tested by China in 2007. The pace of these counterspace efforts appears to be accelerating and the impact of the use of counterspace likely would be felt by all sectors of the space community.

A few examples of existing counterspace weapons and their impacts: Global Positioning System and communication satellite jammers can deny use of essential navigation, timing, and long-distance communication services. Advanced anti-satellite weapons capable of reaching all our orbital altitudes, including the orbits of our critical missile warning and strategic communication satellites, can destroy a satellite and create dangerous orbital debris. And the higher the altitude of engagement, the longer that debris will remain in orbit.

Ground-based lasers can temporarily blind various optical sensors on satellites and other nations are looking to increase the laser power to destructive levels.

Our space capabilities also are reliant on ground stations and cyber connectivity. The ground stations scattered around the world monitor satellite health, receive mission data from these satellites, and send operating commands to those satellites. Without the ground stations, the satellites would not be capable of accomplishing their intended purpose. The possibility of physical attacks on these satellites is certainly a concern.

Equally concerning in this information age is the possibility of cyber attack. With cyber activity occurring at the speed of light, damage can be done very, very quickly. And attributing the activity to a particular actor is often very difficult and time-consuming.

The environment of space has fundamentally shifted then from the ethereal sanctuary of the past to the increasingly crowded and contested environment of today. Broad agreement on this fact, however, has not produced the architectural change decisions to reduce those vulnerabilities.

A recent analysis by the Cost Assessment and Program Evaluation [CAPE] team in the Office of the Secretary of Defense found that space research and development [R&D] is at a 30-year low. The space industrial base is eroding due to this low level of investment. At a time when the space industry's engineering talent and innovation should be put to work, decisions to initiate new programs that are responsive to the threats have not been made.

Understandably, industry is unwilling to invest internal R&D funds until the government makes those decisions. Because satellites have limited lifetimes, the lack of a decision to make needed changes to our architectures due to the changed space environment is a de facto decision to continue the status quo with no additional meaningful protection for our critical space assets.

The last administration began initial steps toward space protection. The relatively new Joint Interagency Combined Space Operations Center has the potential to be a catalyst for how operations in a contested environment must evolve. Experimentation and eventually realistic operational exercises will produce revelations about operating in this new era of space.

But exercises alone won't be enough if the systems in space are not built with prediction and mission resilience as key performance requirements. There simply will be no levers to pull to defend.

To this point, the CAPE analysis found that of the $6 billion added for additional space protection in the 2016 President's budget, approximately 80 percent is currently allocated to non-satellite programs.

Warfare in space is in no one's best interest. And the level of the United States dependence on space means we have the most to lose. As we consider space capability protection options in space, in cyber, and on the ground, we must consider whether our actions are stabilizing or destabilizing in the international arena.

Every action we contemplate should cause us to ask ourselves if said action dissuades and deters potential adversaries from nefarious activity. We urgently need sponsors and funded study work on what constitutes deterrence in the 21st century and what recommended steps would increase our deterrent posture.

We need to think our way through this maze, which requires that we deter use of space and cyber weapons while continuing to deter use of nuclear weapons. The potential consequences are just too great for us to merely hope for the best.

Many of us remember the tag line from the 1979 movie, "Alien": "In space, no one can hear you scream." From my perspective, apparently no one on earth can hear you scream about space vulnerabilities either. Many have banged the gong very hard since 2007, but 10 years of innumerable studies and policy debates have not produced tangible improvements in our space protection posture.

If you know the armed burglar is on the front porch, you don't wait until he is already inside to take action, yet that is precisely our posture today.

I thank the two committees for delving into this subject, and I look forward to answering your questions.

[The prepared statement of General Shelton can be found in the Appendix on page 33.]

Mr. ROGERS. Admiral Allen.

STATEMENT OF ADM THAD W. ALLEN, USCG (RET.), MEMBER, GPS ADVISORY BOARD, FORMER COMMANDANT, U.S. COAST GUARD

Admiral ALLEN. Thank you. Chairman Rogers, Chairman Donovan, Mr. Garamendi, I want to thank you very much for having us here today.

Let me first associate my remarks with General Shelton. I take objection to nothing he has said and wholeheartedly endorse his comments related to space.

I will make mine additive so we aren't duplicative here at the hearing today. And what I would like to do is focus on the civil users segment of GPS.

I serve on the Position, Navigation, and Timing [PNT] Advisory Board to the GPS EXCOM [Executive Committee]. That is the governing entity for GPS in the country, that is co-chaired by the Deputy Secretary of Defense and the Deputy Secretary of Transportation.

The PNT Advisory Board is a subject matter expertise group that provides them recommendations. Many of my comments today and recommendations are grounded in conversations that have been held in public fora associated with that advisory committee and reflect my peers and our collective view of the threats and vulnerabilities and what to do about them moving forward.

What I would like to do is talk about vulnerabilities related to GPS in a little bit more detail and offer a strategy on how we might want to proceed that has been well-discussed, at least among my peer group.

We need to understand in addition to the comments made by yourselves and General Shelton the ubiquity of GPS chips and receivers. They basically permeate all critical infrastructure. This is an issue for homeland security. And in addition to the examples already given, it is the phasing of electrical generation distribution and down to the microsecond as you noted in financial transactions.

The father of GPS is generally regarded as Dr. Brad Parkinson, a professor emeritus at Stanford who I work with on the PNT Advisory Board. And he, together with our peers, have come up with a strategy that I would like to go over with you today that talks about the vulnerabilities and where we might go with them.

Let me just quote Dr. Parkinson first, though: "The first prerequisite for GPS-based position, navigation and timing is a receivable, clear and truthful (truthful implies full integrity) ranging signal, and the second is satellite geometry for the user who cannot see enough of the sky."

The second challenge really requires a denser constellation of satellites and I will talk about the larger, global, navigational satellite system later.

But in regard to the five challenges, the challenges related to availability, let me just talk about five challenges that we have put forward.

First is adjacent spectrum interference. Power signals in adjacent bands to GPS can drown out the signal denying use. In some cases, this is caused by FCC [Federal Communication Commission] authorized users where the implications of licensing decisions are not understood or issued with insufficient testing.

There is natural interference from phenomena such as solar flares.

There is inadvertent, natural or man-made jamming. These are cases where use nearby can cause spurious or destructive emissions.

There is collateral interference. These are privacy devices individuals use to shade where they are at. They can interfere with GPS signals as well.

And then finally, deliberate jamming or spoofing.

In looking how to deal with these threats to GPS, my body recommends, and I recommend personally in my personal capacity, a strategy of protect, toughen, and augment. I would like to break that down to three segments for you, sir.

First on protect, we need to protect the signal. We need to protect the signal and the delivery system. We need to create a deterrent to illegal jamming. We need to control the manufacture and web sale of jammers, which is pretty unabated right now. We need to improve jamming detection. We need to be able to localize and pinpoint jammers. And to the extent that we can eliminate jamming altogether, we should try and do that and that means to be able to find and fix inadvertent or illegal jamming.

And finally, where we have reason to believe that laws have been violated, we need to prosecute offenders and set up consequences for these actions.

Regarding toughening, we need to toughen receivers. There is a number of ways we can do that. Some receivers can be toughened by merely shading through barriers any nearby interference. There is something called signal beam steering by antennas where you basically separate the beams, but it is expensive to toughen receivers this way and it creates a huge expense for ordinary users.

We can integrate GPS with other navigation tools, such as inertial systems. There is always the option to increase GPS signal power, but that is not likely due to expense. GPS was created with a very low signal decades ago without the thought that it would ever be as ubiquitous as it is now and the signal would be put at risk.

And finally, you can separate the GPS signals to allow more effective and discrete processing.

The third PTA, protect, toughen and augment, is augment and by that means to augment the signal itself. One way is to start looking at the international global navigation satellite systems. And that would be Galileo, GLONASS, the Russian system, and the Chinese BeiDou system, and see where we can create compatibility, interoperability, or interchangeable systems.

There also is something called pseudolites or pseudo-satellites which are ground-based equivalent performance of satellites. However, they are limited in their range and they cause frequency interference as well.

And finally, eLORAN [Enhanced Long Range Navigation]—eLORAN is a terrestrial system. It was a system largely in use before GPS was created. It is a high-power, low-frequency signal that can follow the curvature of the Earth. It can also penetrate urban canyons where there are problems with GPS.

In 2009 when I was the commandant and the new administration came in, there was a decision taken to effect cost savings and we terminated the upgrade of the existing LORAN-C [LORAN Revision C] or any development requirements for eLORAN, contrary to domestic agreements that had been made and international agreements that we would pursue this.

We have been in an 8-year hiatus and now there is active discussion about whether eLORAN is a competent terrestrial backup to GPS. My counsel to these committees are that the time is over for talking about this. We need to make a decision and move on.

And I would be happy to answer any questions.

[The prepared statement of Admiral Allen can be found in the Appendix on page 45.]

Mr. ROGERS. I thank you for that statement.

And now we turn to Mr. Nimmich for his opening statement.

STATEMENT OF HON. JOSEPH NIMMICH, FORMER DEPUTY ADMINISTRATOR, FEDERAL EMERGENCY MANAGEMENT AGENCY

Mr. NIMMICH. Good afternoon, Chairman Rogers, Chairman Donovan, and Mr. Garamendi and the other distinguished members of the subcommittee. Thank you for the opportunity to testify about the critical role of satellite technology and preparing for, responding to, recovering from, and mitigating both natural and man-made disasters.

The use of satellites and satellite-derived data is mission critical for emergency management operations. Emergency managers require extensive, timely, and accurate information to make critical lifesaving and life-sustaining decisions.

The decision-making information comes from a multitude of sources with satellites being one of the most critical. Satellites, both national and commercial, inform almost every aspect of emergency management, allowing responders to act faster, smarter, to preserve the safety and security of the American public.

The National Weather Service depends on weather satellites to monitor and collect information about evolving weather systems that are the primary cause of natural disasters. These include tropical systems, tornadoes, flash floods, winter storms, dust storms, volcanic eruptions, forest fires, and geomagnetic space storms to help forecasters predict future weather events and increasing accuracy.

I am going to deviate from my comments to talk about what just was occurring last night and will occur today in the Midwest, Texas, and Louisiana. Those tornadoes were predicted 3 days ago by our weather services. That allowed emergency managers to be prepared for, put extra staff on, and to alert the American public in those areas at a much better and more lifesaving capability.

Emergency managers require these short- and long-term forecasts to carry out their missions. Advanced knowledge of incoming storms, as I just discussed, allows leaders and emergency managers to pre-position assets in a safe location to provide assistance to mitigate the impacts of both river flooding and storm surge, the two most life-endangering events.

Satellites provide critical communication and coordination for response operations. Data and voice communications are the nervous system of an effective response. During disasters, commercial communications are often severely overloaded.

In spite of the overtaxed lines, national satellite communications ensures emergency responders are able to continue to communicate and maintain connectivity at all times. Emergency managers across the country rely on the national communications capability during the most severe events.

Satellite data preserves one of the most valuable resources in emergency management: time. Time, and more specifically advance warning, is the difference between life and death in many events. Local emergency managers can order evacuations based on solid predictions supported extensively by satellite data.

Emergency managers and city planners utilize satellite data in developing and maintaining critical evacuation routes. While evacuations are synonymous with hurricanes, new satellite technology is also improving predictive capabilities to support flash flooding and evacuations and tornado events. Evacuation planning for man-made catastrophes is also ongoing.

This advance knowledge allows FEMA to pre-position assets, build accurate staffing models, and more precisely allocate limited resources to where they are most needed and rapidly adjusts to ever-changing situations. The ability to pre-position resources and make real-time adjustments is critical to an effective emergency response that saves lives.

Satellites are also critical to local, State, and Federal recovery missions. Satellite imagery and geospatial analysis has enabled FEMA to accurately determine house-to-house damage assessments and expedite millions of dollars of rental assistance to disaster survivors. This capability reduces the cost to the taxpayer as damage assessments can be derived from satellite imagery at a fraction of the cost of ground inspections. In some cases, up to 90 percent less costly.

A single satellite image can cover hundreds, even thousands of square miles and provide cheaper and timelier data to deployed teams, especially in remote areas.

I cannot leave my comments allowing you to think that without satellites there would be no response to disasters. Every level of emergency management prepares for emergency response where there is limited access to information, including satellite information and communications capability. But to be very clear, responses to emergencies with degraded satellite information will be less timely, less capable, less efficient, and less effective.

Satellite supports every aspect of emergency managers' efforts to prepare for, mitigate against, respond to, and recover from disasters confronting our Nation. It is critical that the Federal Government continue to invest in these capabilities and ensure their reliability if we are to support the American people in their time of greatest needs.

Thank you for this opportunity to testify today, and I look forward to answering your questions.

[The prepared statement of Mr. Nimmich can be found in the Appendix on page 57.]

Mr. ROGERS. I thank all of you for those opening statements.

I now recognize myself for questions.

General Shelton, I think I know the answer to this, but for the record, are we moving as a nation at the speed we need to in order to address the threats you laid out in your opening statement? And if not, why not?

General SHELTON. Congressman, let me take you back to 2007. I was the commander of 14th Air Force at Vandenberg. We were monitoring the Chinese ASAT [anti-satellite weapon] test in progress. And I was in my operations center, and I watched that successful engagement. And I don't remember if I said this out loud, but I pushed back from the table, and I said the world just changed because that is not a simple engineering feat. And yet, here we are 10 years later and we don't really have a whole lot to show but a pile of studies for our protection posture.

And I really think there are three things here. I think there are some policy decisions that need to be made. Our policy is actually pretty permissive, but we need to make those policy decisions at the highest levels to commit to protecting our space assets.

There are also funding constraints. You know, I mean, that is the age-old story for all of you, but we do have via sequestration, via some other priorities, some constraints on how much money is available to spend on satellite protection.

And we have also been part of this "one more study" kind of attitude. Well, that may not be the perfect answer, so let us just do one more study. And meanwhile, time marches on. And as I said in my written statement, since satellites have fixed lifetimes and you need to plan for the death of a satellite, a decision not to move forward is a de facto decision to maintain the status quo with no additional protection.

Mr. ROGERS. Mr. Nimmich and Admiral Allen, in your experience, does the left hand know what the right hand is doing in the United States Government regarding space threats and dependence? For instance, the Department of Defense knows that there are threats and are working to address them.

However, to what extent does the Department of Homeland Security and FEMA and other appropriate organizations, to what extent are they aware and are working to ensure that they can execute their missions when necessary?

Admiral ALLEN. Sir, with all due respect I would say left hands and right hands. As we move forward, I would just underscore what General Shelton said regarding the one more study. We have become very effective at miring problems in this country. We have governing processes that don't have a clear lead agency for developing requirements where the programs of record should be for funding.

And in my view, until we start to address the overall structure of how we govern, these things are going to continue to have a discussion over whose base is the funding going to come from, who should lead the study, how do we develop requirements. And if you put on that gaps created by changes of administration, this drags on and on and on.

And I think it is time, if we are going to be serious about it, we have to look at the governing process that can produce answers more quickly.

The government has always had a problem in adjusting and deploying technology. But at the rapid rate of advancement, especially with the capabilities of our adversaries, we are in a stern chase and following further behind unless we revisit how we are actually going to make these decisions.

Mr. NIMMICH. Sir, my experience in DHS [Department of Homeland Security] would indicate that they don't own them, therefore they look for somebody else to be able to ensure their operability.

As Admiral Allen pointed out, I think one of the challenges you have got with satellite and space-based capability is the fact that there is no specific critical infrastructure section inside DHS. And the structures, the way they look at critical infrastructure, it is embedded across all of the different critical infrastructure. Therefore, it becomes harder to focus on.

But I would tell you that it is, again, a consumer mentality that we are consuming the capabilities that are provided by others, both commercial as well as national assets. But we are expecting those people that provide them to provide the reliability and the defenses against them.

Mr. ROGERS. I thank you.

The Chair now recognizes Chairman Donovan.

Mr. DONOVAN. Thank you, Mr. Chairman.

Admiral Allen you pointed out something we in Congress could do about the jamming devices.

You have mentioned many challenges, the three of you, the entire panel. What are some of the steps that you think Congress should take to address some of the challenges that each of you have pointed out during your testimony?

Admiral ALLEN. There are a number, but let me just focus on a couple that would almost appear to be simple. The first one is easy access to jammers via the internet. A lot of these actions are illegal, but hardly enforceable. This requires a unity of effort across government. We have just spoken about that. It also requires a level of cooperation between the departments and agencies and the independent regulatory authorities, such as the FCC and the FTC [Federal Trade Commission], moving forward.

But the whole issue of widely available jammers, lack of prosecution or consequences associated with their use, and then the ability for those to be in the hands of either folks that are involved in criminal activity or terrorism, is a clear vulnerability that we should address. And if I were to focus anything specifically, it would be that.

And the second one is adjacent spectrum inference which is another issue regarding signal-to-noise ratio and whether or not GPS signals can be disrupted.

But the availability of jammers, I think, is something we have to address.

Mr. DONOVAN. General.

General SHELTON. Yes, sir. This is going to sound incredibly naive to you, but I think the executive branch and the legislative branch could get together and agree on a strategy and a way forward and then move out and execute.

I don't see any other way. There has to be some broad agreement here in the whole of government as we move forward.

Mr. DONOVAN. Thank you, sir.

Mr. NIMMICH. Sir, I think one of the things when we look at FEMA and the challenges we face is try to eliminate single points of failure. We are talking about jammers and signal strength, but the potentials of a geomagnetic storm taking out entire swaths of satellite capability exists.

I think that we do need to look at a backup system of some sort, whether it be LORAN-E or some other capability. But we have put all of our eggs in one basket and that basket is fragile.

Mr. DONOVAN. That was actually my next question to you. In the case of a disruption in our capabilities, our first responders have backup methods in order to efficiently or as efficiently as they can—I know you mentioned in your testimony one of the things if the systems go down is going to be the time in which they could react or the time in which they get advanced notice of those tornadoes that you spoke about. Do we have backup systems in place?

Mr. NIMMICH. So responders, first responders and emergency managers responded to disasters before there was satellite capability. Satellite capability has enhanced and improved all of the responses as you have pointed out, Chairman.

And what we do is we continue to ensure that we have the proficiency in those pre-satellite capabilities. If GPS goes down, can we use the national grid and train our people both at the State, the local, and the Federal level to be understand what the national grid is and we exercise those. Cascadia Subduction Zone, 2015, national level exercise, used national grid capability.

We look at the redundant capabilities that HF allows us in communications, HF frequency communications, high-frequency communications. That has been tested all the way down to the amateur radio operators who are some of probably the most proficient and the most wide-ranging across this country.

In that same exercise, NORTHCOM [U.S. Northern Command] worked with FEMA to be able to have members of the national amateur radios actually engage with us and provide information that came up.

So there are systems that allow us. They are not as efficient. They are not as effective. They don't take away duplication of effort, so there would be a slower response no matter how you look at it, sir.

Mr. DONOVAN. And your recommendation would be that we invest in a backup system?

Mr. NIMMICH. I think anything that provides the ability, not just from the response side, but the recovery piece. And I think we mentioned in the chairman's office the fact that most of the individual assistance, you are well aware in Staten Island, the number of people that were either left homeless or didn't have resources, the Federal Government provides a certain level of resource up to about $30,000. That is all done electronically. And if GPS fails and there is no timing mechanism, then those transfers don't go into their accounts and now we worry about life-sustaining capability, not just lifesaving capability.

Mr. DONOVAN. I thank you all for your testimony and your response to my questions.

Thank you. I yield the rest of my time, Chairman.

Mr. ROGERS. Thank the gentleman.

The Chair now recognizes Mr. Garamendi.

Mr. GARAMENDI. The members of your subcommittee, Mr. Chairman, are well-aware of where I am likely to take this conversation to eLORAN. And so my apologies to all of them for once again raising this issue.

For Mr. Donovan and your committee, you may not have had the opportunity to be so bored as I carried on about this issue. But we have been at this some time, principally from the Coast Guard and Maritime Subcommittee side of it, which actually happens to be in the Homeland Security Department and so there is interaction there.

General Shelton, you laid out very well in your testimony the overarching situation we are faced with, the dependence on satellites, the vulnerabilities that they have. And we have heard that repeatedly from you and from your successors in our subcommittee.

So I really want to go to Admiral Allen here and the rest of you can chime in along the way.

Your testimony is a little different than most of what we have heard. You actually are suggesting solutions.

And I believe, General Shelton, you have told us very clearly that it lies in decisions that have to be made.

And just running through the recommendations that you have made, Admiral Allen, I am going—protect the signal, jammers, there ought to be a law. There ought to be a law. It ought to be illegal, and certainly that would come under the Homeland Security Committee.

And there are four different recommendations here. Some are different, but they basically say there ought to be a law. If you have a jammer, it is illegal to use it and it is illegal to manufacture and sell it and you are going to get prosecuted. That is something we can do. And I must tell you, it is very important.

Well, since my cellphone is actually working on the internet here, I could probably order up a jammer legally and probably put this entire committee out of commission with that jammer.

Toughen receivers, these are rather important things, all of which can be done. Physical barriers to the receivers, whomever that receiver is that has that, they should be aware and they should deal with it.

Augmenting the signal gets me to where I really want to go. And this is something that we have dealt with many times in committees, in various committees actually.

Some of these have all been discussed, but here we really need a decision. And last year in the transportation legislation, we passed out of this House a decision to move to the eLORAN system and to go with a public/private partnership to make that happen. It did not survive the conference, unfortunately. I think people who know me know that I am going to try again on this one.

But basically it sets up a mechanism for the home security secretary and the commandant of the Coast Guard to put together a request for proposal for a public/private partnership that would build out the eLORAN system.

The eLORAN system, and, General Allen, I am going to leave it to you to describe because I could not do it nearly as well as you could, could you please describe how an eLORAN system could be built in the United States?

Admiral ALLEN. Yes, sir.

Mr. GARAMENDI. And then how that might be able to be accomplished.

Admiral ALLEN. Let me describe what LORAN is. LORAN is a hyperbolic aid to navigation, a signal that is transmitted, high-power, low-frequency, follows the curvature of the earth. A second signal is transmitted. When you receive both of those signals, you take the difference between them, and I am oversimplifying this, and it puts you on a hyperbole between the two points and multiple lines give you a position.

eLORAN is an advancement of this basic technology, it has been around since the end of World War II, that would allow additional information to be transmitted with a signal, a higher degree of accuracy and then produce the three things that GPS does produce, position, navigation, and timing. It does require the construction of terrestrial antennas, big, large radio stations, if you will, to be able to transmit that signal.

We were actively looking at this in 2009 and with the change of administration it was decided that the eLORAN program would be terminated as a cost efficiency. And again, as I noted in my written testimony, we are at a point now where we are actually starting over again where we were 8 years ago.

Mr. GARAMENDI. There are three different parts to this: position, timing, navigation. The timing is essential for the operation of virtually everything, from the electrical grid to cellphones and ATM [automated teller] machines and the like. Positioning and navigation are an additional that GPS adds. Can we do an eLORAN system for timing only and then add to it later the position and navigation?

Admiral ALLEN. You can, sir. There is a timing signal that is being transmitted from a tower in Wildwood, New Jersey, right now to test just that, the timing signal. Yes, sir.

Mr. GARAMENDI. What would it take for those signals, both timing, position, and navigation, to be built into one of these or ATM machines or whatever else?

Admiral ALLEN. That is a little bit of a different challenge, sir, because we stopped building LORAN receivers when there was no signal to be received. There has been some talk in Europe and some movement to combine both eLORAN over there and Galileo which is their global navigation satellite system or their equivalent of GPS.

One might envision in the future with advances made in computation and [miniaturization] that you could hold an eLORAN receiver and GPS receiver in the same device for a redundancy. Right now if you are using an iPhone 6 or above, you have both a GPS chip and Russian GLONASS chip in it to ensure redundancy and reliability.

And I might add that we need to take a look at how we interface with these other systems and how we bring it into a situation where we can assure reliability and signal integrity and take advantage of those signals as well.

Mr. GARAMENDI. Final question and this goes to General Shelton.

How important is a backup system to the work that you did before you retired?

General SHELTON. Sir, we tried to have backups to everything we did.

Mr. GARAMENDI. We have done some studies of this in committee and hopefully I don't get out of bounds here, but it seems to me that in the command and control of the nuclear weapons system that backups are exceedingly important. And without going into any of the detail, could the eLORAN system be a backup system at least for some of those command and control mechanisms?

General SHELTON. You know, sir, I couldn't answer that on a technical level. Maybe Admiral Allen could. But as I understand eLORAN, it is more about navigation and timing and less about direct communications.

Mr. GARAMENDI. It is a very powerful, low-frequency radio signal capable of transmitting data and information one way. Is that correct, Mr. Allen?

Admiral ALLEN. Yes, sir.

Mr. GARAMENDI. Excuse me, Admiral.

Admiral ALLEN. It is all right. I was a commanding officer of a LORAN-C station in Thailand in the war in Vietnam. And information has since been declassified. There was actual work being done on whether or not you could augment a LORAN signal for a fleet broadcast to naval units who are operating in the area. So it has been demonstrated you can use a LORAN signal to transmit command and control information.

Whether or not that is the solution for the nuclear enterprise I don't want to comment on that, but it has been demonstrated that signal can be used as a communications channel as well.

Mr. GARAMENDI. And my final is my own comment. To do the navigation timing, we could do it with a public/private partnership. The Federal Government could or could not engage, but it is about somewhere south of a hundred million dollars to set it up. And that is for the timing issue that allows these things to operate, not your location and your mapping wouldn't, but at least you can do your ATM work remotely. That is a cheap solution on one of the pieces of it.

Admiral ALLEN. Yes, sir. This is not a technology issue.

Mr. GARAMENDI. Thank you. Thank you very much for the time.

Mr. ROGERS. The Chair now recognizes the gentleman from Oklahoma, Mr. Bridenstine, for 5 minutes.

Mr. BRIDENSTINE. Well, thank you, Mr. Chairman.

I wanted to focus, Admiral Allen, on your position on the PNT Advisory Board. You mentioned that some systems use pseudolites. Can you tell us, does the U.S. GPS constellation take advantage of pseudolites?

Admiral ALLEN. They are available and they have been proposed. My understanding is, and I am not going to get in over my depth of water here, my technical background, pseudolites are limited in their range because they are terrestrial based and the amount of power needed can cause disruption with GPS signals. I think it is a general consensus opinion of the folks that I talk with that that would not be a suitable backup.

Mr. BRIDENSTINE. Can you tell me if the BeiDou system operated by the Chinese, does that use pseudolites?

Admiral ALLEN. Not directly. But since you mentioned BeiDou, there is an issue about whether or not we want to take an international look at all of these global navigation satellite systems and see if we can come up with some common way to create interoperability and whether or not these signals can be used for redundant and backup purposes for the other signals.

I think the leading candidate to do that right now would be Galileo, the European Union system. But the international governance structure over the top of this is maturing as well. And there are some options we could explore internationally, but it has been limited to date.

Mr. BRIDENSTINE. Well, let me ask, you mentioned pseudolites as one of the augmentation capabilities that might help mitigate whether it is jamming or spoofing or some other signal problem that you have with GPS. Do you still believe that?

Admiral ALLEN. In my testimony I listed it only because for the purpose of discussion we have looked at all possible areas where you could protect, toughen, or augment the signal. Pseudolites are a way to augment the signal, but the downside associated with that in terms of coverage area and the amount of power that is used makes it not an advisable backup.

Mr. BRIDENSTINE. So does anybody use pseudolites right now as an augmentation that you know of?

Admiral ALLEN. Oh, I think there are pseudolites being used, but I don't think it is in any type of a coherent government structure.

Mr. BRIDENSTINE. Okay. General Shelton, do you have thoughts on that?

General SHELTON. Well, the only thing I would say in addition to what Admiral Allen said was, one of the problems with the GPS reception is it is easily blocked by big buildings or canyons on earth or mountains, you know.

Mr. BRIDENSTINE. The site of your aircraft.

General SHELTON. Exactly.

Mr. BRIDENSTINE. Yes.

General SHELTON. So if you have got a ground-based attempt at augmentation here, like he says, the coverage isn't very great, plus you have got these potential interruptions in the coverage, you know, just due to geography or buildings or whatever.

Mr. BRIDENSTINE. Okay.

Admiral ALLEN. Within the level that we can talk about in this room here, there are localized augmentation options that are being looked at for in-theater loss of GPS for operations. But probably not the focus of this hearing.

Mr. BRIDENSTINE. When we talk about eLORAN, as Mr. Garamendi was talking about, we think about it being maybe a solution to maybe if you lose GPS. At the same time, can you—I mean, right now, of course, our systems aren't designed for it. But if they were, could you use eLORAN in order to, you know, to drop a JDAM [Joint Direct Attack Munition], a precision-guided munition.

Admiral ALLEN. I would defer to General Shelton.

General SHELTON. First you would have to figure out how you are going to receive that signal for a signal that is really intended for kind of nap-of-the-earth coverage as opposed to coming from space.

Mr. BRIDENSTINE. So when we drop a GPS-guided weapon, we have very precise measurements that come from the Geospatial-Intelligence Agency and we are able to know that we have a designated mean point of impact and there is a certain circular error probability for every weapon that we drop that we know we are going to hit that target.

If we went with eLORAN, I would imagine none of that exists, none of that has been tested or proven, which means that it wouldn't necessarily be perfect, although certainly being able to navigate is important. But using it for precision-guided munitions would probably not be something we would be able to do for a number of years.

General SHELTON. Significant testing program would be required, no doubt.

Admiral ALLEN. If I could just add, my comments were directed at the civil user community.

Mr. BRIDENSTINE. Oh, okay, civil user, got it.

Well, a couple of other things. As far as remote sensing for FEMA when we talk about ultimately if there is some kind of natural disaster, we have to figure out what happened and get the right information to the right people.

A lot of the satellites that do that remote sensing are commercial nowadays. And of course, the Geospatial-Intelligence Agency has a huge, you know, desire to have more information, more data.

One of the challenges we have and one of the reasons I think the National Space Council would be so important is because we need to get those satellites licensed quicker. They are being licensed, of course, by NOAA [National Oceanic and Atmospheric Administration], but they have DOD [Department of Defense] implications, they have FEMA implications. There is a whole-of-government challenge here, an interagency problem that we have to deal with. So that is another topic.

And I would leave this with Chairman Donovan and Chairman Rogers. We have heard General Shelton talk about this being infrastructure. This is an important point that General Shelton made, that space is now infrastructure just like the grid. And when we do an infrastructure bill, which I know the President wants to do an infrastructure bill and it seems to be that there is bipartisan support for that, I think space ought to be a big part of that infrastructure bill.

And with that, I will yield back.

Mr. ROGERS. Thank the gentleman.

The Chair now recognizes the gentleman from Rhode Island, Mr. Langevin, for 5 minutes.

Mr. LANGEVIN. Thank you, Mr. Chairman.

I want to thank our witnesses for your testimony and also for your service to the Nation and the various contributions you have made to keeping us safe.

So following on the issue of critical assets, so cyber exploitation of our critical infrastructure is one of the greatest threats to our Nation as I see it right now and that we face as a country today. And in your testimonies, you have alluded to the fact that our satellites and space assets should in fact be included in this category and that we must protect, toughen, and augment these assets.

So what actions have we taken to ensure that we are protecting these critical assets? And how are we mitigating our risk and preventing against cyber attacks on our satellites?

General SHELTON. I think the satellites themselves are very secure. Without going into any detail on that, I think the satellites themselves are well-protected from cyber attack.

The ground stations, however, are an avenue of attack for a potential adversary. We have done everything we know to do to harden those ground stations against cyber attack. But as we have seen in many instances, there are cyber surprises. And so to take any comfort in the fact that our hardening has been a forever fix, so to speak, I don't think that is the appropriate attitude.

Continuing to improve cyber defenses at all our satellite ground stations has got to be a priority.

Mr. LANGEVIN. So one of the things that I am greatly concerned about is miscalculation on behalf of our enemies and adversaries, that they might think of our satellite architecture as assets where they could take action as sending a message or thinking that it is a standoff action that would help to deescalate a situation, where in fact those are critical national assets that we depend on and that we would see as, I believe, a red line.

Do you think that we have done enough to convey to our enemies and adversaries what critical national assets these are and that we will use all assets of national power to protect them and that were they to take action against one of these assets that we would consider it more than just a deescalatory action or that it is expendable, but it is something that we would respond to very harshly?

General SHELTON. Sir, that is a very interesting question. And during the Cold War, there was if not explicit, there was certainly implicit agreement that certain satellites were strategic assets and you didn't do anything to interfere with their operation. That was at least a tacit agreement between us and the Russians.

I don't believe that same level of agreement exists with the Chinese. We have seen in their public writings that they consider this just as another opportunity to take away a strategic advantage that an adversary would have.

Our policy is very clear. We do say very clearly in national space policy that we consider an attack on those assets as vital interests. So it is not prescriptive, it is not an if/then statement, but it is fairly clear in diplomatic language what we mean by that.

Mr. LANGEVIN. Thank you.

To the panel, I also feel strongly that our satellites are like flashlights in the dark, that they are allowing us to see what is not readily observable using traditional technologies, particularly when it comes to climate damage.

How does climate damage threaten our national security interests? And how do our space-based systems and data-driven tools help FEMA to evaluate the threat and prepare for it?

Mr. NIMMICH. Sir, as you know, the nature of the rising sea level as well as the climatic differences that are causing massive rain events that have not been realized before are causing extensive damage to both individual as well as national capabilities.

We use an awful lot of the climatology information that is provided by satellites, as well as satellite use in terms of being able to determine where the risk will be in the future. So we are working closely with NOAA in terms of surge modeling that didn't exist before so that we can actually identify what the storm event may cause damage, flash flooding, and others through our risk map programs and just looking at the natural transition that is occurring in terms of the nature of the storms that are there.

So the ability to understand future impacts along our coastal and our most vulnerable cities and infrastructure are exactly what we are using.

Mr. LANGEVIN. Thank you. Admiral, did you have anything to add?

Admiral ALLEN. The whole notion of sensing is something that we are coming to grips with in the complexity we are dealing with with increasing interaction between the built environment and the natural environment. We are seeing, as Admiral Nimmich said, events of greater frequency and greater consequence and greater scope and scale.

Space-based technology have the opportunity to help us out in some other ways. It is possible with GPS signals to detect very small changes in elevation and other parameters that would give us a warning that there might be seismic activity or even the density of water vapor might help us predict storms. So this is all something that is there, we can use it, and we need to move forward very aggressively and employ it.

Mr. LANGEVIN. Very good. Thank you all for your testimony. And I yield back.

Mr. ROGERS. Thank the gentleman. The Chair now recognizes the gentleman from Florida, Mr. Rutherford, for 5 minutes.

Mr. RUTHERFORD. Thank you, Mr. Chairman.

And thank you, gentlemen, for your testimony today.

I go back to something that General Shelton said earlier about Congress and the executive branch getting together and moving forward and defining roles. And you talked a little bit about responses, Admiral Allen did.

Oddly enough, that was one of the things that came out in a discussion about cyber attacks and warfare, too, is this inability to really define whose roles and responsibilities are at play in protection and prosecution and those things.

I would ask, we talked about the government response, I was wondering in this, like in the cyber world, where does private industry, what responsibilities do they accept when they go into space?

Admiral ALLEN. Let me talk on the user side and then maybe General Shelton would like to comment.

Mr. RUTHERFORD. Thank you.

Admiral ALLEN. There are very few critical infrastructures that don't have embedded GPS receivers someplace. And so you need to talk about the responsibility of the private sector in carrying out their own enterprises and basically standard of care if you will.

In this case, GPS PNT issues and cyber issues are not that far apart. We are operating in an area where the technology is advancing. We are operating in an area where some of the legal frameworks for international cooperation and what constitutes, say, an act of war or a crime are not as clear and we are faced with the challenge of defending, protecting, and even using offensive operations simultaneously in the same environment. Very, very confusing moving forward.

But from the civil side, there is a discussion going on right now with Homeland Security and the critical infrastructure sectors about what it means to have vulnerabilities in industrial control systems and other areas where you have GPS receivers that, if they were denied that service or spoofing or jamming, what it might do to that critical infrastructure sector. And I think that is a current focus, but it needs to be continued.

Most of those upgrades to reduce those vulnerabilities don't happen unless it is part of an operations maintenance cycle because there is no monetary incentive for companies to do that and we have to change that.

Mr. RUTHERFORD. Thank you, sir.

General SHELTON. Sir, I think a good analogy is the maritime domain. You know, people operate in the maritime domain, they don't have any defensive capability, they don't worry about protection. They count on host-nation support and the United States Navy support for U.S.-flagged vessels.

Same thing in space, I think. Private industry is not concerned about coming under attack because they think we are going to provide the protection for U.S. assets. And unfortunately right now, it is just not so.

Admiral ALLEN. If I can maybe just add another comment. And I will try and quote, I may not do it exactly right, our former colleague, Keith Alexander. He and I were on a panel last week when the notion of common defense came up as defined in the Constitution. I think we are seeing a re-definition of what that means.

In the past, a banking system didn't seem to be something that would be critical to national security. But if you look at the implications of loss of time and what might happen to the banking system or cyber denial of service or other attacks, I think we are re-shaping what actually the common defense means and what our responsibilities are related to that. And it is a conversation that is in progress.

Mr. RUTHERFORD. Thank you, sir.

And I would also just make an observation that when we talked about the jamming and those who have been prosecuted and really the lack of significant penalties going along with that, we see the same thing on the cyber side.

And I really think, Mr. Chairman, this is one area where Congress should certainly step up and address the lack of real penalties for some of these violations, particularly in the finance and commerce world, but also in protecting our space assets as well. And I think that is something that we should, as legislators, should certainly be looking at very strongly.

Would you support that concept?

Admiral ALLEN. Yes, sir. Let me just make sure I was clear on my comments. There are some penalties associated with the illegal activities. The question is, are they significant enough to deter activity? Are they enforceable? And do we have a unity of effort in how we are addressing the problem?

And all of that, in my view, speaks to room for improvement.

Mr. RUTHERFORD. General Shelton.

General SHELTON. Interestingly enough, GPS jamming has been used to block criminal activity, you know, put a jammer in place so the criminal can't be tracked. So, yes, sir, more penalties would be a good thing.

Mr. RUTHERFORD. Thank you.

Mr. Nimmich, did you want to comment on that?

Mr. NIMMICH. It really doesn't fall under emergency management in that regard, sir. But clearly, one of the challenges you have gotten in past experiences, it is not just the penalties, but the infrastructure to be able to identify where the jammer is and take action to prevent that jammer. We still have not developed the countermeasures for jamming that are necessary to maintain the reliability of the system.

Mr. RUTHERFORD. Thank you, Mr. Chairman. I yield back.

Mr. ROGERS. Thank the gentleman.

The Chair now recognizes for a closing question the gentleman from California, Mr. Garamendi.

Mr. GARAMENDI. I noticed Mr. Cooper just arrived, so I am going to make this a very quick question.

Mr. Bridenstine raised the question of the potential for eLORAN in a military situation. There are some systems that could work, but I don't see how they would work for the precision munitions that you might fly on your plane. But there are some ground-based systems out there that are either in place or about to be put in place.

But the eLORAN is basically continental United States and Alaska and it could be offshore. It goes about a thousand miles offshore.

But my question is this and this is part of what Mr. Bridenstine was going at and that is positioning. Can eLORAN give an accurate position? We know that its timing is nearly as accurate or is as accurate as GPS, but how about positioning and navigation? If it were established within the continental United States, could it give good positioning and navigational work?

And I guess to any of you, but let us start with Admiral Allen and then the rest of you can jump in.

Admiral ALLEN. It could. The level of accuracy related to LORAN has to do with the physical parameters of the distance between the antenna and the reception. So you would have to decide, what would be the level of reliability and signal strength and accuracy that you wanted. The more accurate you get, the more sophisticated and expensive the system is going to be to do that.

But we are looking at ability to back up the GPS when it is needed. And I think that would have to be discussed. You can crank that down to a pretty fine degree of accuracy, but there is a question of cost and the infrastructure that would be required to support it.

Mr. GARAMENDI. And that is really the number of towers that you would place and where you would place them.

Admiral ALLEN. That is correct. And if I could just add on, you were correct earlier, the current version of the eLORAN system would be for the U.S. area to basically provide a backup in that area below the GPS coverage that is current in the GPS. You could conceivably have a global backup system, but that would be an extensive, extensive eLORAN system.

Mr. GARAMENDI. I yield back my time. I see my colleague has arrived, he seems to have been satisfied listening in on all of this.

Mr. ROGERS. Well, I want to thank the witnesses for your participation today. This has been a very important topic to help us focus on it also, but raise awareness that we need to be taking some action. So thank you for being here and your participation.

And with that, we are adjourned.

[Whereupon, at 3:11 p.m., the subcommittees were adjourned.]

APPENDIX

MARCH 29, 2017

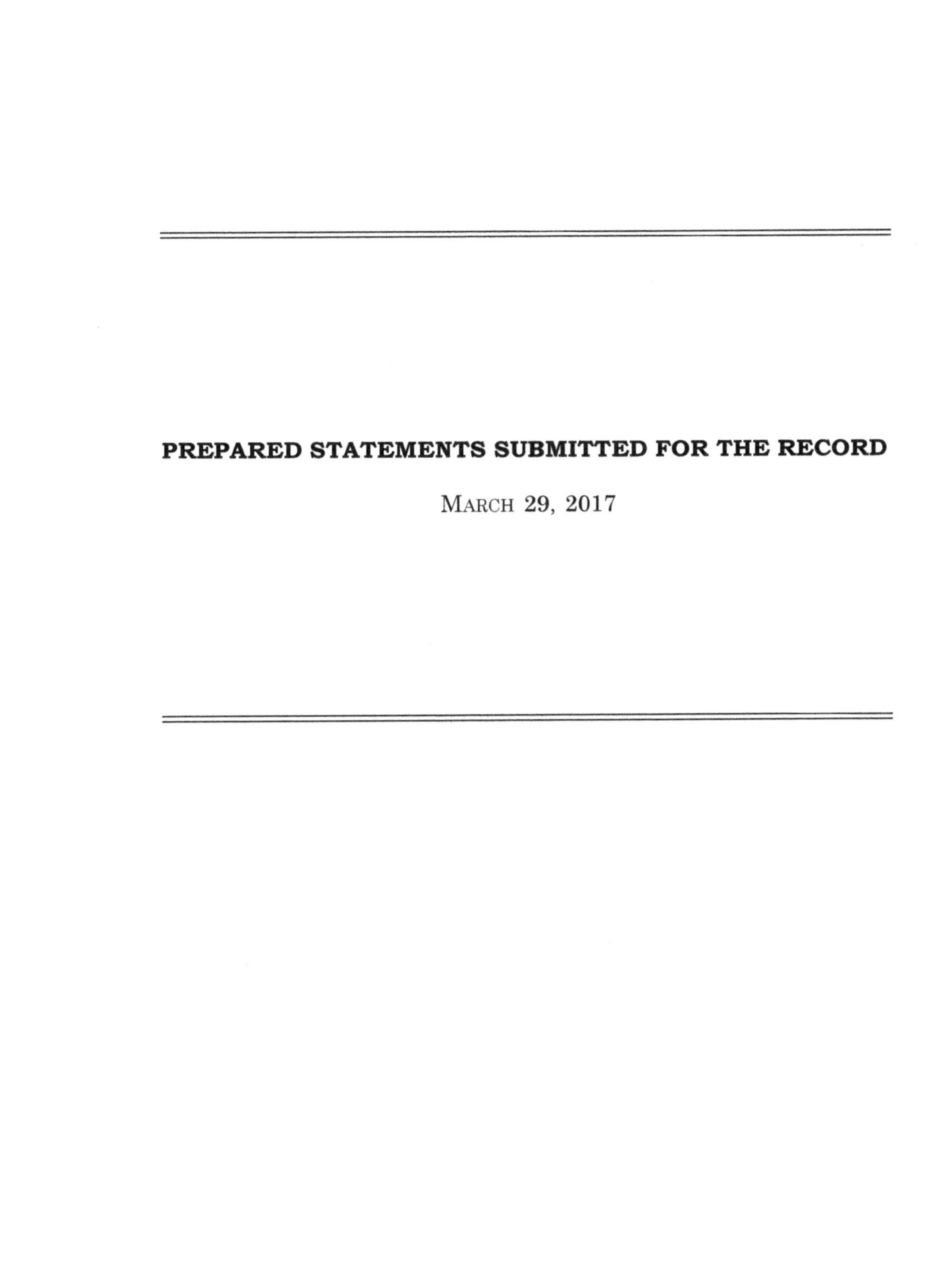

PREPARED STATEMENTS SUBMITTED FOR THE RECORD

MARCH 29, 2017

Opening Remarks – As Prepared for Delivery
The Honorable Mike Rogers
Chairman, Subcommittee on Strategic Forces
House Armed Services Committee
Hearing on the "Threats to Space Assets and Implications for Homeland Security"
March 29, 2017

Good afternoon and welcome to the hearing on "Threats to Space Assets and Implications for Homeland Security" held jointly by the House Armed Services Subcommittee on Strategic Forces and the Homeland Security Subcommittee on Emergency Preparedness, Response, and Communications.

I want to start by thanking our witnesses for their distinguished careers in public service.

We have an expert panel with us regarding the topics of space and homeland security. Though testifying in their personal capacities, they each have decades worth of experience dealing with the issues being discussed here today.

Our witnesses are:

General William Shelton, retired Air Force and
Former Commander of the U.S. Air Force Space Command

Admiral Thad Allen, retired Coast Guard and
Member of the GPS Advisory Board and
Former Commandant of the U.S. Coast Guard

The Honorable Joseph Nimmich
Former Deputy Administrator, Federal Emergency Management
Agency (FEMA) and Retired Rear Admiral, U.S. Coast Guard

I also want to thank Chairman Donovan and Ranking Member Payne for supporting this joint hearing.

We have heard extensively from Department of Defense and Intelligence Community officials regarding the potential foreign threats to our space systems. The threats are real, serious, and only getting worse.

Unfortunately, talking about a conflict extending to space isn't science fiction anymore.

And the impact of that threat extends beyond the military.

It extends to our way of life here in the United States.

There likely isn't a person in this hearing room, nor within this entire Capitol campus, that hasn't utilized the services provided by satellites at some point today.

For instance, aside from DirectTV and Dish satellite TV – which allow me to watch Alabama play football on Saturdays no matter where I am..Roll Tide! – the Global Positioning System, or GPS, is probably the most widely known space asset and for good reason.

While I think many recognize that GPS powers their navigation in their cars and cell phones, they may not recognize the support it provides to financial transactions, farming, shipping, public safety, environmental monitoring, and a host of other areas.

The American public may also not realize that GPS is built and operated by the United States Air Force -- potential adversaries recognize our dependence on it.

I guarantee for you that.

And GPS is one of the many important space systems.

We spend time in the Armed Services Committee understanding what the loss of space would mean to the military, and the need to protect and defend these systems.

But what does the loss of space mean to our economy and financial institutions?

Or our agricultural activities?

Or transportation infrastructure?

Today, our witnesses will help us understand the importance and role of space regarding our homeland security and our emergency response.

The public deserves to know what is at stake when we're talking about the risk of loss of our access to space.

It's my sincere hope that a conflict never reaches into space, but conflict has extended across air, land, sea, and cyberspace. Hearings like this one are needed to make sure we're aware of the consequences we now face if it ever does happen, and ensure we are ready for it.

Statement of Subcommittee Chairman Dan Donovan (R-NY)
Emergency Preparedness, Response, and Communications
Subcommittee

Joint Hearing with the Armed Services Committee's Strategic Forces
Subcommittee

"Threats to Space Assets and Implications for Homeland Security"

March 29, 2017

Remarks as Prepared

Good afternoon. First, I would like to thank Chairman Rogers for holding this hearing today and including my Subcommittee in this very important and timely discussion.

In today's world, our lives are connected more than ever before and this is because of our space-based capabilities, specifically satellites. Without satellites, we cannot:

- Make financial transactions
- Communicate with cellphones
- Navigate from one location to another
- Fly airplanes
- Watch television; and
- Effectively prepare for and respond to natural disasters and, god forbid, terrorist attacks.

Space-based capabilities, like Global Positioning Systems (GPS), satellites communications, and remote sensing, not only help our military operations but have made it safer for our first responders to effectively and efficiently respond to a crisis or emergency.

Nearly five years ago, my district, which includes Staten Island and parts of Brooklyn, was devastated by Superstorm Sandy. This "perfect storm" caused dozens of New Yorkers to lose their lives, thousands of homes to be damaged or destroyed, and for billions of dollars to be spent on reconstructing communities, including my own.

The preparedness and response efforts directed at Superstorm Sandy, while not perfect, were much better than previous major disasters, like Hurricane Katrina. Satellite capabilities were part of the reason first responders and government agencies had the information needed to respond decisively and quickly.

Satellites are being used to enhance our nation's preparedness and response efforts, especially when critical infrastructure is damaged, destroyed, or overloaded. I saw this firsthand during Superstorm Sandy.

Prior to Superstorm Sandy making landfall, the Federal Emergency Management Agency (FEMA) used the storm track predications from weather satellites to preposition equipment and resources all along the east coast. Additionally, FEMA used satellite imagery to expedite the disaster declaration process and provide assistance to impacted areas. During the response effort, teams deployed satellite communications equipment and high-throughput satellite terminals to provide voice and internet connectivity to first responders and survivors. These are a few of the growing reasons why satellite capabilities are key to our homeland security.

While we need to continue to look for ways to incorporate space-based capabilities into our preparedness and response efforts, we need to be cognizant of the threat to these space systems. There are numerous threats, whether intentional to naturally occurring, that could damage or destroy our satellites and significantly reduce the life-saving capabilities they provide to our first responders. I'm particularly interested in learning more about how our nation's preparedness and response efforts could be impacted if our space capabilities were diminished.

I want to thank our distinguished panel for testifying this afternoon and I look forward to learning more about what we, in Congress, can do to help ensure our military and first responders don't lose these vital capabilities.

I yield back the balance of my time.

Opening Statement of Ranking Member Donald M. Payne, Jr. (D-NJ)

**Subcommittee on Emergency Preparedness, Response and Communications
Joint Hearing**

Threats to Space Assets and Implications for Homeland Security

Wednesday, March 29, 2017

Almost five years ago, Hurricane Sandy slammed into the East Coast, wreaking havoc on critical infrastructure – including the communications systems first responders and emergency managers rely on for planned and unplanned events.

"Satellite broadband service" supported voice and data connectivity at FEMA Disaster Recovery Centers and "communications and broadband Internet service" was critical to Habitat for Humanity's rebuilding effort in Breezy Point, New York.

But one of the most important factors that made the Federal response to Hurricane Sandy so much better than its response to Hurricane Katrina was its forward thinking approach – its actions before the storm hit.

That pro-active approach was facilitated by weather satellites that gave emergency managers at the Federal, State, and local level the information they needed to execute evacuation plans, secure infrastructure, and pre-position critical assets.

Today, satellite technology provides resiliency to the Emergency Alert System and 9-1-1 public safety answering points, ensuring emergency responders' ability to warn the public early and the public's ability to call for help when they need it.

In New Jersey, the emergency communications system developed with our NTIA B-TOP grant, known as "JerseyNet," leverages satellite technology to provide resiliency for voice and data capabilities on its deployable system-on-wheels.

But even as we rely on satellite technology to improve the resiliency of emergency communications systems, those systems are themselves vulnerable to physical and cyber attacks by state and non-state actors.

The potential disruption and harm that such an attack could do to critical infrastructure, in particular maritime and aviation systems, are particularly troubling.

In 2013, a man used an illegal GPS jamming device in his truck to hide from his employer. This activity interfered with the satellite-based tracking system at Newark Liberty International Airport that is essential to tracking a plane's location in the air and on the runway for air traffic controllers. Fortunately, the incident did not endanger any flights and no one was injured, but we were lucky.

Emergency managers need to understand the vulnerabilities that exist in their own communities. Today, I will be interested in understanding what we can do to help first responders understand the threats to the satellite technologies as well as the vulnerabilities such threats may create in their own communities.

Joint Hearing Statement
Bennie G. Thompson (D-MS), Ranking Member, Committee on Homeland Security
Threats to Space Assets and Implications for Homeland Security
Emergency Preparedness, Response & Communications Subcommittee
March 29, 2017

I represent the Second Congressional District in Mississippi. Over the past 15 years, my district has experienced devastating floods and debilitating tornadoes and has even survived the impact of Hurricane Katrina. Unfortunately, there is no indication that these storms are letting up—in fact, these weather events may end up becoming increasingly frequent and severe.

More and more, the people in Mississippi and along the Gulf Coast will rely on satellite technology to forecast the path of dangerous storms, inform evacuation activities and routes, and strategically pre-position assets for disaster response. In the aftermath of storms, satellites will provide surge capacity capabilities for emergency communications, and can improve connectivity in rural environments.

Given the increasingly prominent role that satellite assets play in our ability to prepare for and respond to disasters, I will be interested in understanding the extent to which the impact of threats to satellite assets are understood by the emergency management community, and the degree to which disaster response plans take into account those threats.

Outside of disasters, commercial satellite assets are important to a range of industries—from banking and agriculture to transportation and broadcasting. As we have witnessed over the past year with Russia's use of cyberattacks to interfere with the 2016 Presidential election, our adversaries are pursuing novel methods of attack in an attempt to undermine our confidence in our economy, our democracy, and ultimately, our way of life.

Certainly, an attack on satellite assets could result in an overwhelming degree of disruption. I will be interested in understanding how threats to space assets —from both State and non-state actors—are communicated to State and urban area fusion centers as well as relevant commercial sectors, and to what degree we are in a position to mitigate potential vulnerabilities. I will also be interested in understanding the full range of threats posed to space capabilities, and what actions Congress should be taking to protect against them.

Statement Before the

House Armed Services Subcommittee on Strategic Forces
and
House Homeland Security Subcommittee on Emergency
Preparedness, Response and Communications

"Threats to Space Assets and Implications for Homeland Security"

Testimony by:

General William L. Shelton, USAF (Ret)

Former Commander, US Air Force Space Command

March 29, 2017

Room 210, House Visitor Center

Shelton: Testimony, House Armed Services Subcommittee on Strategic Forces and House Homeland Security Subcommittee on Emergency Preparedness, Response and Communications, 3/29/17

Chairman Rogers, Chairman Donavon, Ranking Member Cooper, Ranking Member Payne and distinguished members of the Committees, thank you for your invitation to appear today to discuss threats to our space assets and the implications of those threats to our homeland security. While on active duty and since I have retired from the Air Force, I have attempted to alert decision-makers to the current and growing threats to national security space systems. I believe the vast majority of Americans are not conscious of these threats, and are therefore blissfully unaware of the impacts on our way of life should conflict extend to space. I commend your committees for taking up this subject.

> *Space products and services are found throughout the economy and society. Although the connection to space may not always be readily apparent, it is now rare for most of us to pass an entire day untouched by space in at least one way.*
> *The Space Report, 2016*
> *Space Foundation*

For most of our citizens, space is synonymous with NASA. Manned spaceflight missions on the Space Shuttle, life aboard the International Space Station, and robotic explorations of our solar system capture imaginations and promote our technical prowess. Dreams of humans going to Mars and beyond motivate private investment and attract young talent to NASA and to entrepreneurial companies involved in space.

Much less publicized, and therefore much less known, is the host of satellites that provide services essential to modern life in the United States and across the planet. In fact, according to the latest edition of The Space Report, published annually by the Space Foundation, the global space industry is a $325 billion business. Satellite-provided services have become analogous to electricity—a utility we take for granted. Most of us don't need to—nor want to—know where or how our power is produced. But we expect our local power company to continuously provide the power we need to heat and cool our houses, and to run our myriad electrical devices. When a power outage occurs, we are outraged and quickly call the power company demanding to know when service will be restored. Space services are now a utility as well. Few Americans understand that fact.

> *The list of human activities that are dependent on space systems contains most of the major functions that are vital to modern society, including trade and commerce; banking and financial transactions (from operations of major financial markets to minor retail purchases); personal, corporate, and government communications; agriculture and food production and distribution; power and water systems; transportation; news gathering and distribution; weather assessment and prediction; health care and entertainment. Were the world to suddenly be "without space," these would all seriously degrade or shut down entirely.*
> *National Security Space Defense and Protection Report*
> *National Academy of Sciences, 2016*

Shelton: Testimony, House Armed Services Subcommittee on Strategic Forces and House Homeland Security Subcommittee on Emergency Preparedness, Response and Communications, 3/29/17

Both military and law enforcement personnel depend daily on satellite services. In fact, it would be difficult for them to execute their missions without space assets because they have become so accustomed to it. The best way to think about this level of dependence is to consider space services as foundational capability. Back to the utility metaphor—we just expect it to be there and thus we take it for granted.

In contrast, potential adversaries are well aware of our dependence on satellites. Continuous combat operations since OPERATION DESERT STORM in 1991 have provided an unparalleled learning laboratory for them. Not surprisingly, nations are now actively testing methods to deny us continued use of space services during conflict. They have developed a full quiver of these methods, ranging from satellite signal jamming to outright destruction of satellites via a kill vehicle, such as that successfully tested by China in 2007. The pace of these counterspace efforts appears to be accelerating, and the impact of the use of counterspace capabilities likely would be felt by all sectors of the space community.

> *In the view of many, space has been, until recently, a "sanctuary" from intentional attack, but that sanctuary status has now eroded or vanished.*
> *National Security Space Defense and Protection Report*
> *National Academy of Sciences, 2016*

> *Threats to our use of military, civil, and commercial space systems will increase in the next few years as Russia and China progress in developing counterspace weapon systems to deny, degrade, or disrupt US space systems. Foreign military leaders understand the unique advantages that space-based systems provide to the United States.*
> *Russia and China continue to pursue weapons systems capable of destroying satellites on orbit, placing US satellites at greater risk in the next few years. China has probably made progress on the antisatellite missile system that it tested in July 2014. The Russian Duma officially recommended in 2013 that Russia resume research and development of an airborne antisatellite missile to "be able to intercept absolutely everything that flies from space."*
> *Worldwide Threat Assessment, US Intelligence Community*
> *Senate Armed Services Committee, Feb 9, 2016*
> *James R. Clapper, Director of National Intelligence*

Following are a few key examples of our dependence on space systems, accompanied by descriptions of how current and developing threats could interrupt, and potentially preclude, our access to satellite services.

- Global Positioning System satellites enable precise navigation and timing services across the world. High speed communications networks, first responder location abilities, cellular phone capability, high efficiency farming, transportation vehicle tracking, and many other applications depend on the signals radiating from GPS satellites. Military operations are heavily reliant on GPS for precision warfare. Unfortunately, GPS jamming capability has proliferated to the extent that relatively low power jammers are now available for sale online. Several nations have developed much higher power jammers, thereby increasing the size of the jammed area and making the jamming effects more difficult to overcome. Widespread and well-conceived jamming during conflict would impact both civilian and military users of GPS.

- Communications satellites in low earth orbits as well as higher altitude orbits provide "over-the-horizon" services at the speed of light. Television, radio, voice, video, financial transaction data, and many other signals are received and relayed continually by satellites. Some of the most important communications networks for national security are dependent on jam-resistant communications satellites. Like GPS jammers, however, proliferation of communications satellite jammers complicates combat mission planning and execution. Also troubling is the development of both low- and high-altitude anti-satellite weapons by China and Russia. Interference or destruction of even one communications satellite likely would open a geographic hole in a constellation, preventing normal communications in that region. This fact holds true for both commercial and government satellites. Until recently, the higher orbits of most of these satellites were thought to be unreachable by potential adversaries' anti-satellite weapons. But continued development and testing by these nations has demonstrated that no orbit can be regarded as safe from attack.

- Missile warning satellites operate at higher orbital altitudes and use infrared sensors to detect heat sources on the surface of the earth and above it. The plume exiting a rocket engine is very hot, which is detected by satellites and transmitted to ground stations. The intensity and length of a rocket engine's burn, as well as the trajectory of the rocket, allows the ground stations to determine the range and type of the rocket. This also enables classification of the rocket type: missile or space booster. Using all this information about the rocket, an assessment can be made on whether an attack is in progress—on the United States' territory, on our allies' territories or on our deployed forces. That data also is used to cue early warning radars and missile defenses. Early warning enabled by these satellites provides the President, allied leadership and operational commanders the maximum time possible to prepare for, and respond to, an attack. Without these satellites, warning times would be limited to the much shorter timelines achievable with the coverage of missile warning radars alone. Clearly, maximizing response decision time is critical and missile warning satellites are the key.

- Imaging satellites provide vital data for earth observation. Optical and radar imaging satellites orbit at lower altitudes and transmit images used for earth resources data collection, disaster relief, intelligence collection, map making, treaty monitoring and many other services. A picture is truly worth a thousand words for a military commander and for a treaty monitor. On the other end of the spectrum, satellite images provide broad coverage to aid disaster response officials, which is particularly important in remote regions. Because of the ability of imaging satellites to collect images over denied territory, they become prime targets for denial and destruction by potential adversaries in times of conflict. Ground-based lasers can be used to temporarily or permanently blind an optical satellite. Radar satellites can be jammed from the ground or from space. And both radar and optical satellites in low orbits are vulnerable to ground-based anti-satellite weapons on a very short timeline: launch to kill in as little as 10 minutes.

- Weather satellites operate at both low and high orbits to collect information on terrestrial weather and solar activity. Sensors on the satellites allow analysis of cloud formations, surface winds, wave heights and other important meteorological data. These data have a direct impact on our national security because they provide advanced warning of storms, thereby preserving human life. Hurricane warnings, for example, enabled evacuations and preparations that have saved many lives in storms such as Katrina and Sandy. Daily forecasts seen on TV and other news sources also depend on satellite data to feed the weather models which produce the forecasts. Solar weather sensors provide important data on high energy particles ejected from the sun. These particles can impact satellite performance, terrestrial communications links, and astronaut and aircrew health. Forecasting of solar storms alerts satellite operators to possible electronic malfunctions, and it allows NASA to implement special protection measures for astronauts in orbit. Weather satellites are vulnerable to the same threats discussed above. In addition, potential reductions in the funding for the next generation of weather satellite programs could create major shortfalls in our ability to provide the warnings and the daily forecasts we now take for granted.

Many other types of satellites, their uses and their vulnerabilities to existing and developing threats could be addressed, but I believe the point is made: space is critical for our economic vitality, for efficiency of modern life and for our national security. It logically follows, then, that protecting our space assets is no longer merely desired—it is essential.

Thus far, I have focused on satellite vulnerabilities. Our space capabilities also are reliant on ground stations and cyber connectivity. The ground stations scattered around the world monitor satellite health, receive mission data from the satellites, and send operating commands to the satellites. Without the ground stations, the satellites would not be capable of accomplishing their intended purpose. The possibility of physical attacks on these stations is a concern. While steps are taken to ensure security to the maximum extent practicable, the stations still are potential avenues of attack on space systems. Equally concerning in this information age is the possibility of cyber attack. Cyber security upgrades have been made at every ground station; however, we should not conclude that cyber attacks are no longer possible. With cyber activity occurring at the speed of light, damage can be done very quickly. And attributing the activity to a particular actor is often difficult and time-consuming.

The increasing number of objects in orbit also presents a threat to our satellites. Active satellites, non-operational satellites, spent rocket stages and other space debris occupy the same orbital regimes. The problem is particularly acute in lower orbits. While the sheer volume of space is immense and the probability of collisions is low, when two objects meet at orbital velocities, the results are catastrophic. A 2009 collision between an active Iridium communications satellite and a non-operational Russian satellite is Exhibit A of the situation. Every collision causes a large increase in debris, which exacerbates the overall space traffic problem. The Chinese anti-satellite test in 2007 resulted in thousands of pieces of debris—

pieces that still represent a navigation hazard today. As the number of objects in orbit increase, and as intentional and unintentional collisions occur, the collision probabilities increase to potentially unacceptable levels. Currently in the planning stages are large constellations of small satellites for imaging and broadband services. These, too, will add to the complex task of space traffic management in the coming years.

> *We have consistently underestimated both the rate of increase in our own space-related capabilities, our reliance on them, and the rate at which potential threats have progressed with the ability to counter them.*
> *Admiral James O. Ellis, Jr., USN (Ret)*
> *Former Commander, U.S. Strategic Command*
> *Testimony to the House Armed Services Subcommittee on Strategic Forces*

The environment of space has fundamentally shifted from the ethereal sanctuary of the past to the increasingly crowded and contested environment of today. Broad agreement on this fact, however, has not produced architectural change decisions to reduce our vulnerabilities. A recent analysis by the Cost Assessment and Program Evaluation (CAPE) team in the Office of the Secretary of Defense found that space research and development is at a 30 year low. Worse, some 15-40% of that amount is used to fund management services and technical assistance functions, not actual program-related research and development. The space industrial base is eroding due to this low level of investment. Further compounding the historically low investments, the engineering staff in the satellite industry has declined by 28% in last decade. At a time when the space industry's engineering talent and innovation should be put to work, decisions to initiate new programs that are responsive to the threats have not been made. Understandably, industry is unwilling to invest internal R&D funds until the government makes those decisions. Because satellites have limited lifetimes, the lack of a decision to make needed changes to our architectures due to the changed space environment is a de facto decision to continue the status quo with no additional meaningful protection for critical space assets.

The last administration began initial steps toward space protection. The relatively new Joint Interagency Combined Space Operations Center has the potential to be a catalyst for how operations in a contested environment must evolve. Experimentation and eventually realistic operational exercises will produce revelations about operating in this new era of space. Developing new concepts of operations and new tactics in the face of extant and postulated threats is essential. The time-honored adage of "train like you're going to fight" applies in space as well. But exercises alone won't be enough if the systems in space are not built with protection and mission resilience as key performance requirements—there simply will be no levers to pull to defend. To this point, the CAPE analysis found that of the $6B added for space protection in the 2016 President's Budget, approximately 80% is currently allocated to non-satellite programs.

*With our newfound appreciation of the importance of space systems, we had
better understand the significant threat to modern society that their loss
represents and, in considering how best to respond, we appreciate both the
urgency of the need and the depth of the challenge. While deterrence, in all its
dimensions, must be part of our national strategy, a successful outcome
nationally and globally requires all elements of diplomatic, intelligence, military,
and economic domains to achieve outcomes desired nationally and acceptable
globally.*

National Security Space Defense and Protection Report
National Academy of Sciences, 2016

Warfare in space is in no one's best interest, and the level of the United States'
dependence on space means we have the most to lose. As we consider space capability
protection options in space, in cyber and on the ground, we must consider whether our actions
are stabilizing or destabilizing in the international arena. Every action we contemplate should
cause us to ask ourselves if said action dissuades and deters potential adversaries from
nefarious activity. Deterrence is successful when an adversary believes we have the strength to
impose costs on them or to deny the benefits they seek. Unfortunately, classical deterrence
theory fails us when our actions are not observable due to orbital distances, cyber anonymity
and/or security classification. We urgently need sponsored and funded study work on what
constitutes deterrence in the 21st century and what recommended steps would increase our
deterrent posture. We need an intellectual framework to think our way through this maze
which requires that we deter use of space and cyber weapons, while continuing to deter use of
nuclear weapons. The writings of Bernard Brodie and Herman Kahn on nuclear deterrence
strategy provide a good model for the intellectual depth needed. That same level of research
from academia and think tanks would help navigate negotiations on international agreements
governing space activity—agreements which are either outdated or sorely lacking. The
potential consequences are too great for us to merely hope for the best.

Some have suggested we just throw in the towel on space. Because space systems are
now being threatened, as their logic goes, we can't depend on them when we most need them.
I strongly reject that argument. The unique and often ubiquitous services available from space
either can't be replicated, or the alternatives are impractical and/or too expensive. We don't
stop operating in any other domain when challenged—we find ways to make our systems
effective while defeating or mitigating the threats. So, we must determine how we will defend
our space systems and make them more mission resilient to interruption, denial and
destruction. And the programmatic decisions to produce a protected space architecture are
long overdue.

*A key aspect of space is that the speed of advances in access and spaceborne
capabilities has significantly outpaced the creation of guiding national-let alone
international strategies and policies. The technological advances in space
systems and increased reliance on them have created a space-enabled "critical
infrastructure" that has not been matched by coherent supporting protection and*

> *loss-mitigation strategies, clearly articulated and accepted policies, and robust
> defensive capabilities.*
>> *National Security Space Defense and Protection Report*
>> *National Academy of Sciences, 2016*

Many of us remember the tag line for the 1979 movie, *Alien:* "In space, no one can hear you scream." From my perspective, apparently no one on earth can hear you scream about space vulnerabilities, either. Many have banged the gong hard since 2007, but 10 years of innumerable studies and policy debates have not produced tangible improvements in our space protection posture. Most would find this inaction intolerable if satellites had mothers. They don't, but America's sons and daughters, as well as society in general, heavily depend on space services—some in life or death situations. If you know the armed burglar is on the front porch, you don't wait until he is already inside the house to take action. Yet that is precisely our posture today.

> *We are living in a paradox: The achievements of the industrial and information
> ages are shaping a world to come that is both more dangerous and richer with
> opportunity than ever before.*
>> *Global Trends Report*
>> *National Intelligence Council, 2017*

Our heavy reliance on space capabilities for modern living, as well as national security operations, creates vulnerabilities to current and escalating threats. Other nations have chosen to create weapons systems with the clear intent of exploiting those vulnerabilities if and when they choose to do so. I believe our nation is more than capable of adjusting to this new environment and protecting our critical space infrastructure while avoiding unnecessary provocation. I thank the two committees for delving into this subject and I look forward to answering your questions.

William L. Shelton
General, United States Air Force, Retired

William Shelton is an independent consultant and a member of the Board of Trustees for the Aerospace Corporation and a member of the Board of Directors for Airbus Defense and Space, Inc. He also serves as Vice Chairman of the Board of Directors for the Space Foundation.

General Shelton retired as Commander, Air Force Space Command, in September 2014. During his career, he commanded space operations units at every level and held staff positions in a wide range of Air Force and Department of Defense organizations. In his final assignment, he led a team of over 40,000 at Air Force Space Command to provide space and cyberspace operational forces as well as acquisition of space systems. In this role, he was responsible for a budget of over $10 billion.

During his career, General Shelton was a Space Shuttle controller for the first 18 missions, commander of Global Positioning System operations during the initial deployment of the constellation, and commander of the largest ballistic missile wing. He also commanded all Department of Defense space operations during internationally significant events such as the Chinese anti-satellite test and the North Korean Taepo Dong launch. He served as the CIO of the Air Force and the director of the Air Force headquarters staff during one of the most turbulent periods in the Air Force's history. While leading Air Force Space Command, he reduced $1 billion from the operations budget while preserving vital space services. He also drove the development of new satellite architectural concepts to address growing space threats and significant fiscal challenges. Finally, he led the rapid maturation of cyberspace forces to enhance both the defensive and offensive cyber capabilities of the Air Force.

General Shelton earned a bachelor of science degree in astronautical engineering from the United States Air Force Academy in 1976, a master of science degree in astronautical engineering from the Air Force Institute of Technology in 1980, and a master of science degree in national security studies from the National War College in 1995.

DISCLOSURE FORM FOR WITNESSES
COMMITTEE ON ARMED SERVICES
U.S. HOUSE OF REPRESENTATIVES

INSTRUCTION TO WITNESSES: Rule 11, clause 2(g)(5), of the Rules of the U.S. House of Representatives for the 115th Congress requires nongovernmental witnesses appearing before House committees to include in their written statements a curriculum vitae and a disclosure of the amount and source of any federal contracts or grants (including subcontracts and subgrants), or contracts or payments originating with a foreign government, received during the current and two previous calendar years either by the witness or by an entity represented by the witness and related to the subject matter of the hearing. This form is intended to assist witnesses appearing before the House Committee on Armed Services in complying with the House rule. Please note that a copy of these statements, with appropriate redactions to protect the witness's personal privacy (including home address and phone number) will be made publicly available in electronic form not later than one day after the witness's appearance before the committee. Witnesses may list additional grants, contracts, or payments on additional sheets, if necessary.

Witness name: William L. Shelton

Capacity in which appearing: (check one)

✓ Individual

___ Representative

If appearing in a representative capacity, name of the company, association or other entity being represented: ___________________________________

Federal Contract or Grant Information: If you or the entity you represent before the Committee on Armed Services has contracts (including subcontracts) or grants (including subgrants) with the federal government, please provide the following information:

2017

Federal grant/ contract	Federal agency	Dollar value	Subject of contract or grant
None			

2016

Federal grant/ contract	Federal agency	Dollar value	Subject of contract or grant
None			

2015

Federal grant/ contract	Federal agency	Dollar value	Subject of contract or grant
None			

<u>Foreign Government Contract or Payment Information</u>: If you or the entity you represent before the Committee on Armed Services has contracts or payments originating from a foreign government, please provide the following information:

2017

Foreign contract/ payment	Foreign government	Dollar value	Subject of contract or payment
None			

2016

Foreign contract/ payment	Foreign government	Dollar value	Subject of contract or payment
None			

2015

Foreign contract/ payment	Foreign government	Dollar value	Subject of contract or payment
None			

Statement Before the

House Armed Services Subcommittee on Strategic Forces
and
House Homeland Security Subcommittee on Emergency
Preparedness, Response and Communications

"Threats to Space Assets and Implications for Homeland Security"

Testimony by:

Admiral Thad W. Allen, US Coast Guard (retired)

Former Commandant, US Coast Guard

March 29, 2017

Room 210, House Visitor Center

Chairman Rogers, Chairman Donavon, Ranking Member Cooper, Ranking Member Payne and distinguished members of the Committees, thank you for your invitation to appear today to discuss threats to our space assets and the implications of those threats to our homeland security. The is topic both timely and complex. I am honored to participate in this panel with my distinguished colleagues, General Shelton and Rear Admiral Nimmich. Given the breadth of knowledge represented by these professionals and the areas they intend to discuss I would like to focus my testimony on global navigation satellite systems (GNSS) which include the US Global Positioning System (GPS) and the threats and vulnerabilities associated with the services provided by those systems – positioning, navigation, and timing services or PNT.

For background, it is important to understand at the most basic level what space means to modern society because it is generally underappreciated and taken for granted, like oxygen. Access to space in our lifetimes has created the means for better communications, better knowledge of the earth and its environment, enhanced ability to know both friend and adversary, and connect societies in ways unimaginable just decades ago. It is undebatable we are a connected society and space is the linking and integrating domain that connects us all, not unlike weather. The ability to operate in space requires physical access and persistent presence, including the ability to communicate with and control assets in space. These elements are generally regarded as the space and ground control segments. The benefit and functionality derived from the space segment is generally divided into government or military users and public institutions and the public at large.

At the heart of this access and associated functionalities that both benefit and threaten its user is the ability to observe and transmit information through increasingly sophisticated sensing and communication platforms. Beyond the physical access to space created by human ingenuity, from Sputnik to deep space exploration, what connects us to space and space to us to is the electromagnetic spectrum. From micro wave and radio communications, to ionizing radiation, to light itself the presence and nature of the electromagnetic spectrum allow the transmission of energy and with it information. Accordingly, it is impossible to discuss the threats to space assets and their associated services without a discussion of electromagnetic spectrum as the unifying enabler in this domain.

As noted earlier, the purpose of my testimony today is to focus on the systems of satellites that provide autonomous geospatial positioning information to receiving equipment by line of sight radio frequency transmissions. Specifically, position (including altitude and elevation), movement or navigation, and time. The generic term for these systems is Global Navigation Satellite Systems (GNSS) indicating they have global coverage to provide autonomous geo-spatial positioning, navigation, and timing (PNT). The Global Positioning System (GPS) is the United States GNSS. Other GNSS include the European Union Galileo, Russian GLONASS, and Chinese Beidou systems, as well as other system that provide limited regional coverage in a particular area.

As noted earlier, the United States' GPS is divided into three segments: the space segment, the ground control segment, and the civil user segment. Today I would like to focus on the relationship between the space segment and the civil user segment and associated vulnerabilities and risks. The US military developed, deployed, and continues to enhance GPS services and, accordingly, General Shelton is imminently qualified to address the remaining portions of the GPS infrastructure.

My testimony today if offered in my personal capacity and I am not representing any government or private sector entity. I would note that I do serve as a member of the Space Based Positioning, Navigation, and Timing Advisory Board (PNTAB) to the GPS Executive Committee, the federal governing body for GPS, that is co-chaired by the Deputy Secretaries of Defense and Transportation.

The GPS system was declared operational in 1993, after an extended period of test, evaluation, and discussion regarding public access to un-degraded GPS services. Since then GPS and GNSS have become ubiquitous in our lives and geolocation and timing services touch every American every day. Combined with advances in computation, miniaturization, access to spectrum, and mobility, GPS devices can be found in almost every electronic component and is the geolocation services backbone for the internet of things. Further, advances in timing technology have allowed GPS timing services, augmented by high performance clocks, to produce measures of time well below the micro second threshold. As a result, GPS is a critical service in ATM operations, the timing of computerized financial transactions, and the synchronization of telecommunications signals and phasing of power generation. Conservative estimates put worldwide GPS users at over 2 billion. Because of its widespread penetration in electronics and other devices the overall value of GPS services is difficult to calculate. Initial forays into estimating this impact have produced estimates from 30 to 90 billion dollars annually and the models continue to be refined. While GPS is not considered critical infrastructure, there is no critical infrastructure that is not dependent on or impacted by GPS, especially "Lifeline Sectors" such as Communications, Energy, and Emergency Services. Homeland Security officials have stated that our adversaries are interested in doing the Nation harm by disrupting GPS signals (Kolasky 2017). Earlier this year Spirent Communications, a leading provider of mobile network services warned of an "likelihood of disruptions this year" to GNSS.

We must keep in mind that GPS was originally designed as a low power, line of sight signal that allowed terrestrial receivers to determine a position on earth. In fact, were it not for the encoding of the signal so that it could located, the signal would be lost in cosmic background noise. The rapid expansion of these services has placed a premium of their value but has also increased the risks associated with a loss or denial of service. The ultimate vulnerability of a weak signal was something not anticipated in the development of GPS but it now a structural part of the service that must be understood and dealt with.

As reported by GPSWORLD.COM in 2014, Stanford Professor Emeritus and an original architect of the US GPS capability opened his presentation at the European Navigation Conference (ENC-GNSS 2014) in Rotterdam, The Netherlands, with the following question, "What can we do to reduce the vulnerability (of GPS) and ensure that the expectations of the public are going to be met?" In 2016, Dr. Parkinson was awarded the Marconi Prize by the Marconi Society recognizing his contribution in the field of information and communication science which benefit humanity.

Dr. Parkinson's presentation has evolved to become the backbone of the strategy to ensure GPS services by the PNTAB in their recommendations to the GPS EXCOM. The strategy revolves around three lines of effort that are needed to create "assured PNT" for all users: Protect, Toughen, and Augment. These lines of effort address two basic features of reliable GPS: signal availability and integrity. The most critical feature to insure service is "availability." That means the availability of a signal at the specified accuracy of the system. The second critical aspect is "integrity." That means the user receives the expected accuracy and the system is not providing false, incorrect, or inaccurate information.

While the public generally associates positioning, navigation, and timing as GPS-related services, Dr. Parkinson would argue that the goal should be to assure public access to all three in a systemic, redundant, and resilient manner. Accordingly, my remarks today align with that construct. We need assured PNT regardless of the source, space based or terrestrial. Further, we need to understand the services available from the other GNSS and their potential to provide redundancy and assured PNT with the overall goal to be the assured availability and integrity of the information.

"The first prerequisite for GPS-based PNT is a receivable, clear, and truthful (truthful implies full integrity) ranging signal … the second is satellite geometry … the user who cannot see enough of the sky."

Dr. Bradford Parkinson, 2014

The second challenge cited above requires a denser constellation and a means to deal with obstructions like urban canyons. Regarding the first, five challenges are presented by Dr. Parkinson:

1. Adjacent spectrum interference: Power signals in adjacent bands to GPS can drown out the signal denying use. In some cases, this is caused by FCC authorized users where the implications of licensing decisions are not understood or issued with insufficient testing.

2. Natural Interference: Phenomena such as solar flares (space weather) can cause signal interference, attenuation, or delays. Progress in tracking these events and improving prediction has been made and the Space Weather Prediction Center has been established by NOAA in Boulder CO.

3. Inadvertent Natural or Manmade Jamming: In these cases nearby devices can create spurious or destructive emissions.

4. Collateral Interference: Many personal privacy devices that are intended to elude geolocation can impact nearby users.

5. <u>Deliberate Jamming or Spoofing</u>: This continues to be a major concern for all developers and users of GNSS.

Protect, Toughen, Augment
(Advocated by Dr. Parkinson and supported by the PNTAB)

<u>Protect the Signal</u>

The first protect element of the PTA strategy to protect the signal and delivery system. This must begin with protection of the spectrum for GNSS operations. Current concerns center on nearby spectrum licensed for broadband use. Satellite based signals are rebroadcast from terrestrial antennas at a much higher power jamming nearby GNSS receivers.

The second protect element is to create a deterrent to illegal jamming by enacting stiff, behavioral influencing penalties in terms of fines and jail sentences. GPS jammers are currently available on the internet. While FCC penalties exist, they are not a credible deterrent and rarely employed.

The third protect element is to control the manufacture and web sale of jammers. The FCC has indicated they are committed to doing this. That commitment needs to be honored.

The fourth protect element is to improve jamming detection. This can involve independent sensors or improvements to firmware and software by manufacturers to create more "competent" receivers.

The fifth protect element is to localize and pinpoint jammers. This technology is advancing and needs to be sustained.

The sixth protect element is to eliminate jammers. We need a committed national effort at the federal, state, and local level to "find and fix" inadvertent or illegal jamming.

The seventh and final protect element is to prosecute offenders. Prosecutorial discretion can be used based on circumstances when warranted but consequences must be equal to the effects cause by illegal intentional jamming.

<u>Toughen Receivers</u>

Advances are being made to toughen or develop more competent receivers. Some techniques can be accommodated in market driven improvements and upgrades. Improve receiver performance should be supported. There are five general options but the goal should be to make these changes/upgrades affordable.

Local antenna shading: The creation of a physical barrier to shield the receiver.

Signal beam steering by antennas: this is an effective but expensive way toughen receivers but creates expense for ordinary users.

Integration of GPS with other navigational tools such as inertial systems

Increased GPS signal power. An option but not likely due to the expense.

Physical separation of the GPS signals to allow more effective, discrete processing.

<u>Augment the Signal</u>

This element of PTA focuses on augmenting or substituting PNT sources to increase redundancy. The first source can be exploiting existing GNSS with all-GNSS receivers that diversify frequencies and signals, thereby reducing vulnerabilities. This approach also addresses the needs of sky impaired users. However, this approach will require international cooperation similar to that historically achieved by the International Maritime Organization (IMO) or the FAA and International Civil Aviation Organization (ICAO) in their domains. International GNSS governance remains a work in progress. Regardless, there is merit to pursuing this course of action with three objectives related to GNSS integrity: compatibility, interoperability, and interchangeable systems. Standards for integrity monitoring need to be developed and implemented.

Receivers can also conduct integrity monitoring if enough satellites are in view. Standardization among GNSS (interchangeability) would enhance this option greatly. Other sources of augmentation and improved signal integrity include:

Global Differential GPS (GDGPS): This NASA administered real time tracking network provides integrity tracking and the ability to augment the signal for improved performance.

Pseudolites: or Pseudo-Satellites. These are ground based transceivers that could provide additional ranging information. However, the coverage is limited and may involve frequency interference with GNSS.

Distance Measuring Equipment (DME): This modernized FAA system supplements GPS for airborne users. However, ground users are limited by line of sight.

eLORAN: This terrestrial system uses a low frequency powerful signal and presents an attractive relatively low cost alternative to assured PTA and is widely supported.

Summary

This testimony regarding the vulnerability of GPS/PNT and the PTA strategy for assuring service is a condensation of extensive work done by others: government, industry, and the PNTAB. My goal has been to summarize the key issues and I do not represent myself as having the technical solutions to all the issues and options raised. I have, however, been involved in operational issues related to radio navigation my entire career, including a tour as Commanding Officer LORAN Station Lampang, Thailand at the close of the war in Viet Nam. From that vantage point I have two closing comments.

As Commandant, I watched as OMB removed Coast Guard funding in 2009 for modernizing LORAN C and potentially developing eLORAN consistent with domestic and international commitments to seek alternatives to back up GPS. With a new DHS Secretary and new administration there was little appetite in 2009 to appeal this arbitrary reduction made under the guise of "cost savings." We are now eight years later poised to reconsider the development of an eLORAN system to support assured PNT. We should make up our minds and finish the job.

At the same time, the overall governance of the US GPS continues under the Executive Committee governance model. Issues regarding adjacent spectrum interference are difficult to address with overlapping roles and responsibilities between the federal agencies and independent regulatory agencies such as the FCC. Spectrum allocation, management, and governance continue to be critical to protecting the GPS signal. As stated in their June 13, 2016 letter to the GPS EXCOM the PNTAB objected use of adjacent spectrum to GPS for wireless terrestrial broadband without testing that satisfactorily meets 6 criteria:

1. Adhere to previous EXCOM guidance to ensure new spectrum proposals "are implemented without affecting existing and evolving uses of space-based PNT services"

2. Strictly apply the 1dB degradation Interference Protection Criterion (IPC)

3. Protect all classes of GPS receivers, including precision and timing receivers.

4. Protect GPS receivers in all receiver operating modes, including signal acquisition/reacquisition

5. Protect all users of all emerging GNSS signals.

6. Use maximum authorized transmitted interference powers and propagation models that do not underrepresent the maximum power of the interfering signal (particularly consider the impact of the multiple transmitters creating additive interference).

The PNTAB further endorsed "the Department of Transportation Adjacent Band Compatibility assessment as the most scientific valid approach to date for Protecting space-based PNT based on the above criteria."

Finally, any infrastructure investment program developed to address the current challenges facing this country, regardless of political origin, should require assured PNT and the associated resiliency as a basic design parameter

My recommendation is that these committees also endorse this extensive work done to date to protect GPS and assure PNT to civil users.

Thank you for the opportunity to testify before this joint hearing today and I look forward to your questions.

Thad Allen

Thad Allen retired from the Coast Guard in 2010 as the 23rd Commandant. He currently serves as Executive Vice President at Booz Allen Hamilton where he supports government and commercial clients in cyber security, energy and the environment, navigation systems, emergency response, and crisis leadership. He is a nationally recognized expert in disaster response and an advisor to government leaders. He was the lead federal official for the responses to Hurricanes Katrina and Rita and the Deepwater Horizon Oil. He also directed Coast Guard operations in the wake of the 9/11 attacks and the Haitian Earthquake. A 1971 graduate of the Coast Guard Academy, Admiral Allen also holds Master Degrees from The George Washington University and MIT Sloan School. He is a member in the Council on Foreign Relations and a Fellow in the National Academy of Public Administration. He serves on a number of federal advisory committees and holds the James Tyler Chair at the Admiral James M. Loy Institute for Leadership at the Coast Guard Academy.

DISCLOSURE FORM FOR WITNESSES
COMMITTEE ON ARMED SERVICES
U.S. HOUSE OF REPRESENTATIVES

INSTRUCTION TO WITNESSES: Rule 11, clause 2(g)(5), of the Rules of the U.S. House of Representatives for the 115th Congress requires nongovernmental witnesses appearing before House committees to include in their written statements a curriculum vitae and a disclosure of the amount and source of any federal contracts or grants (including subcontracts and subgrants), or contracts or payments originating with a foreign government, received during the current and two previous calendar years either by the witness or by an entity represented by the witness and related to the subject matter of the hearing. This form is intended to assist witnesses appearing before the House Committee on Armed Services in complying with the House rule. Please note that a copy of these statements, with appropriate redactions to protect the witness's personal privacy (including home address and phone number) will be made publicly available in electronic form not later than one day after the witness's appearance before the committee. Witnesses may list additional grants, contracts, or payments on additional sheets, if necessary.

Witness name: Thad Allen

Capacity in which appearing: (check one)

☒ Individual

☐ Representative

If appearing in a representative capacity, name of the company, association or other entity being represented: ____

Federal Contract or Grant Information: If you or the entity you represent before the Committee on Armed Services has contracts (including subcontracts) or grants (including subgrants) with the federal government, please provide the following information:

2017

Federal grant/ contract	Federal agency	Dollar value	Subject of contract or grant
None			

2016

Federal grant/ contract	Federal agency	Dollar value	Subject of contract or grant
NONE			

2015

Federal grant/ contract	Federal agency	Dollar value	Subject of contract or grant
NONE			

<u>Foreign Government Contract or Payment Information</u>: If you or the entity you represent before the Committee on Armed Services has contracts or payments originating from a foreign government, please provide the following information:

2017

Foreign contract/ payment	Foreign government	Dollar value	Subject of contract or payment
NONE			

2016

Foreign contract/ payment	Foreign government	Dollar value	Subject of contract or payment
NONE			

2015

Foreign contract/ payment	Foreign government	Dollar value	Subject of contract or payment
NONE			

Written testimony of former FEMA Deputy Administrator Joseph Nimmich for a joint House Armed Services, Subcommittee on Strategic Forces; and, House Homeland Security, Subcommittee on Emergency Preparedness, Response and Communications hearing titled "<u>Threats to Space Assets and Implications for Homeland Security</u>."

Good afternoon, Chairman Rogers, Chairman Donavon, Ranking Members Cooper and Payne, and members of the subcommittees. My name is Joseph Nimmich and I am the former Deputy Administrator of the U.S. Department of Homeland Security's (DHS) Federal Emergency Management Agency (FEMA). Thank you for the opportunity to testify today about the critical role of satellite technology in preparing for, responding to, recovering from, and mitigating disasters.

The use of satellites and satellite-derived data is mission critical for emergency management operations. Emergency managers require extensive, timely, and accurate information to make critical life-saving and life-sustaining decisions. Their decision-making information comes from a multitude of sources, with satellites being one of the most critical. Satellites, both national and commercial, inform almost every aspect of emergency management, allowing responders to act faster and smarter to preserve the safety and security of the American public.

U.S. Government's Satellite Capability

Emergency managers work closely with the National Oceanic and Atmospheric Administration, or NOAA, when preparing for potential storms. NOAA operates the Nation's system of environmental satellites, including "geostationary operational environmental satellites", or "GOES," for short-range monitoring and warnings; as well as "polar-orbiting environmental satellites", or "POES," for long-term forecasting. Local, state, and Federal emergency managers all rely heavily on NOAA's satellite data.

NOAA's satellites track weather events, including tropical systems, tornadoes, flash floods, winter storms, dust storms, volcanic eruptions, and forest fires. NOAA also monitors space weather events, such as geomagnetic storms, which can disturb Earth's magnetic field and communications networks. The ability to monitor this second category of storms is critical in reducing damage to public infrastructure systems, including power grids, telecommunications, aviation, and GPS.

The National Weather Service depends on weather satellites to monitor and collect information about evolving weather systems to help forecasters predict future weather events with increasing accuracy. Emergency managers require these short- and long-term forecasts to carry out their mission. Advance knowledge of incoming storm systems allows the government to preposition assets in a safe location or provide assistance to mitigate the impacts of river flooding and storm surge.

<u>Satellite Data for Before, During, and After an Event</u>
In addition to satellite-supported weather forecasts, emergency managers utilize satellite-based sensors for critical information regarding the atmosphere, earth's surface, and our built environment. This information is utilized by decision-makers at all levels to enact timely decisions both in the immediate as well as the long term.

Pre-Disaster Mitigation
One of the most significant ways communities can prepare in advance of a storm is through pre-disaster mitigation efforts. These efforts can include basic preparations such sandbags and hurricane shutters, but the most effective forms involve community investments in long-term projects, such as: constructing safe rooms in areas prone to tornadoes; building homes and infrastructure outside of flood-prone areas; and enforcing stricter building codes in areas at risk of earthquakes to ensure structures are built to withstand aftershocks. Smart mitigation is informed by risk, and determining accurate risk requires an understanding of the changing environment over time.

FEMA monitors urban and infrastructure changes over time through a robust archive of historical and current satellite images. These images provide a baseline for investments in mitigation efforts that protect our nation's critical infrastructure. FEMA's flood mapping relies heavily on satellite-derived elevation data for advanced flood modeling, flood zone designation, flood insurance updates, and flood map production.

Satellites also enable smarter prepositioning, which in dire circumstances, can be the difference between life and death. Satellites inform more efficient routing of Urban Search and Rescue teams, supply convoys, and the proper positioning of supply distribution points. As an example, during Hurricane Matthew, risk maps helped FEMA leadership predict the extent and location of damages well in advance of the storm's landfall. This advance knowledge allowed FEMA to preposition assets, build accurate staffing models, and more precisely allocate limited resources to where they were most needed. The ability to pre-position resources is critical to a prompt emergency response.

Emergency managers and city planners also utilize satellite date in developing and maintaining critical evacuation routes in high-impacted communities. In instances of hurricanes or flash flooding, models such as HURREVAC incorporate real-time satellite information to allow local and state officials to order timely evacuations. Early warnings of pending tornados by satellite-supported models provide effected individuals the minutes needed to relocate to safe rooms and interior shelters.

Response and Recovery

The best response to a disaster starts well before the disaster actually occurs. Early and accurate predictive information supported by satellite data allow emergency managers to move people, responders, and commodities in advance of the storm, saving lives in the face of disasters.

Satellite data preserves one of most valuable resources in emergency management: time. Time, and more specifically, advance warning is often the difference between life and death. Local emergency managers can order evacuations based on solid predictions supported extensively by satellite data. While evacuations are synonymous with hurricanes, new satellite technology is also improving predictive capabilities to support flash flooding evacuations and tornado events. Evacuation planning for manmade catastrophic events is ongoing.

Satellite technology also improves response time. In the immediate hours after a storm, satellite imagery provides the foundation for the whole community's common operating picture. Information from meteorological, atmospheric, and imaging satellites contribute to situational awareness of unfolding or impending impacts, allowing for more timely evacuation and deployment decisions. This imagery can assist decision-making by identifying the extent and impacts of flood inundation; locating and analyzing debris fields; and assessing patterns of damage within disaster areas to identify areas of greatest need. Satellite imagery also helps in detecting and assessing road, bridge, airport, and port damages, and in characterizing impacts to critical infrastructure, public buildings, and dwellings.

Satellite imagery can quickly confirm areas of worst impact and need, and help focus the timely delivery of aid to survivors. During Hurricane Sandy, rental assistance was expedited to over 44,000 applicants whose home were identified as inaccessible through remote sensing and geospatial analysis. Imagery-derived damage assessments speed approval of Presidential declaration decisions and deployment of national assets. All of this helps us to more quickly and efficiently locate and serve survivors in the hours and days after a storm.

Satellites are also critical to local, state, and federal recovery mission. Satellite imagery and geospatial analysis has enabled FEMA to accelerate house-by-house damage assessments and expedite millions of dollars of rental assistance to disaster survivors. This capability reduces costs to the taxpayer, as damage assessments can be derived from satellite imagery at a fraction of the cost of ground inspections, in some cases up to 90% less costly. A single satellite image can cover hundreds, even thousands of square miles and provide cheaper and timelier data than deployed teams, especially in remote areas.

Finally, satellites provide critical communications and coordination for response operations. Data and voice communications are the nervous system of any effective response. During disasters, commercial communications are often severely overloaded. In fact, many of you may recall the 2011 Virginia earthquake that was felt here in Washington, D.C. As you may remember, within minutes, it was impossible to make commercial calls or send text messages as the system exceeded capacity. In spite of the overtaxed lines, satellite communications ensured emergency responders were able to continue to communicate and maintain connectivity at all times. Much like that day, emergency managers across the country rely on this national communications capability during the most severe events.

Satellite Technology in Action
Before I conclude, I'd like to discuss the role of satellites in the last major response I supported as FEMA Deputy Administrator, the response to Hurricane Matthew.

Information on the potential severity of Hurricane Matthew began coming in weeks before landfall. On September 28, NOAA began monitoring a tropical storm off the African coast, and original predications indicated it could eventually impact the Southeastern United States.

In the eleven days leading up to landfall, NOAA's satellite data allowed the emergency management community start to plan for eventualities. As the storm progressed, iterative models from NOAA satellites indicated predicting a 90-degree change of course, resulting in significant impacts to the Florida coastline. This information allowed FEMA to engage Florida early on, determining the potential impact and resources necessary to address potential impacts.

As Matthew roared across Haiti, preparations in Florida were well underway. The President declared an Emergency Disaster Declaration, which allowed the Federal Government to provide emergency funding and resources in support of the State. Commodities such as generators, food, water and personnel were made available, and the Governor ordered evacuations of highly susceptible coastal populations.

As Matthew approached Florida, real-time satellite data improved projections and determined the hurricane would not make landfall, but instead stay just offshore. This change in projection refocused our efforts, and the response focus moved to Georgia and South Carolina. Both Governors requested, and the President granted, Emergency Disaster Declarations and with the stroke of a pen, Federal focus rapidly moved to these states. The states ordered evacuations of at-risk coastal areas and awaited the storms arrival. Utilizing satellite communications and GPS capabilities, FEMA moved commodities no longer needed in Florida to Georgia, South Carolina and North Carolina. The rapid changing environment was met with a rapidly adaptive response, all enabled by the use of national and commercial satellites.

On October 8, Hurricane Matthew came barreling into Georgia overnight, making landfall near McClellanville, S.C, about 35 miles northeast of Charleston, and worked its way up the coast. The storm weakened throughout the day and it became clear that the most significant impacts would be inland flooding. North and South Carolina, having been inundated by rain just a week prior, knew the stream and rivers couldn't absorb the near 15-20 inches of rain Hurricane Matthew would create. While it seemed as though the worst had passed, we knew significant flooding was imminent.

Using information from RiskMAP, State and Federal Emergency Managers were able to project those areas most likely to be severely flooded. Since we were already aware of the shift in weather patterns, resources originally planned for Florida were already on their way to North Carolina. Commodities were provided to support shelters for those forced out of their homes. Generators were available to support critical infrastructure. And most importantly personnel were in place ahead of the flooding, to preserve life and property. Urban Search and Rescue teams with fast water capabilities were in the right place at the right time, thanks to reliable satellite information and effective coordination and communication. Soon after the hurricane passed, federal disaster declarations were swiftly approved based on imagery-derived damage assessments, allowing survivors to begin the road to recovery. The use of satellite technology provided the data necessary to expedite the timely delivery of aid to survivors.

CONCLUSION

I will conclude with this: I cannot leave this discussion with readers thinking that without satellites there would be no response to disasters. Every level of emergency management prepares for emergency response where there is limited access to information including satellite information. But to be very clear responses to emergencies with degraded satellite information will be less timely, less capable, and far less efficient. satellites are the bedrock of efficient emergency response. They support every aspect of Emergency Managers' efforts to prepare for, mitigate against, respond to, and recover from disasters confronting our nation. It is critical that the federal government continue to invest in these capabilities if we are to support the American people in their times of greatest need.

Thank you for the opportunity to testify today. I look forward to any questions the subcommittees may have.

Joseph L. Nimmich was confirmed by the United States Senate as the Deputy Administrator of the Federal Emergency Management Agency (FEMA) in September of 2014 serving until January 2017. During his tenure, his primary focus is on strengthening and institutionalizing the Agency's business architecture over the long term to achieve the FEMA mission.

Under his leadership, the Agency has undertaken a number of efforts, including actively modernizing FEMA's information technology systems, instituting data analytics to enable evidence-based decision making, enhancing communication, and building a broader and more diverse workforce. In addition, Mr. Nimmich played an instrumental role in establishing and facilitating several Agency governance structures that provide FEMA's program offices with a practical and collaborative approach to identify inefficiencies and gaps in decision- making, the ability to make decisions strategically and transparently, and in a manner that benefits the organization as a whole.

Mr. Nimmich joined FEMA in 2013, as the Associate Administrator for the Office of Response and Recovery. He was responsible for directing the Response, Recovery, and Logistics Directorates, as well as the Office of Federal Disaster Coordination. Additionally, he was responsible for coordinating and synchronizing all of FEMA Headquarters' operational response activities during major disasters and/or emergency activations.

Prior to joining FEMA, Mr. Nimmich was the Director of Maritime Surveillance and Security at the Raytheon Corporation, where he directed maritime surveillance and security operations, as well as their emergency response capabilities. He served in the U.S. Coast Guard for more than 33 years, retiring as a Rear Admiral. His Coast Guard assignments included the First Coast Guard District based in Boston, Massachusetts, where he was responsible for all Coast Guard operations across eight states in the northeast and 2,000 miles of coastline from the U.S.-Canadian border to northern New Jersey.

Mr. Nimmich earned his Master's in Business Administration from the Stern School of Business at New York University and holds a Master's Degree in Strategic Studies from the U.S. Army War College. He received his Bachelor of Science Degree in History and Government from the U.S. Coast Guard Academy.

DISCLOSURE FORM FOR WITNESSES
COMMITTEE ON ARMED SERVICES
U.S. HOUSE OF REPRESENTATIVES

INSTRUCTION TO WITNESSES: Rule 11, clause 2(g)(5), of the Rules of the U.S. House of Representatives for the 115th Congress requires nongovernmental witnesses appearing before House committees to include in their written statements a curriculum vitae and a disclosure of the amount and source of any federal contracts or grants (including subcontracts and subgrants), or contracts or payments originating with a foreign government, received during the current and two previous calendar years either by the witness or by an entity represented by the witness and related to the subject matter of the hearing. This form is intended to assist witnesses appearing before the House Committee on Armed Services in complying with the House rule. Please note that a copy of these statements, with appropriate redactions to protect the witness's personal privacy (including home address and phone number) will be made publicly available in electronic form not later than one day after the witness's appearance before the committee. Witnesses may list additional grants, contracts, or payments on additional sheets, if necessary.

Witness name: Joseph L. Nimmich

Capacity in which appearing: (check one)

☒ Individual

☐ Representative

If appearing in a representative capacity, name of the company, association or other entity being represented: ____

Federal Contract or Grant Information: If you or the entity you represent before the Committee on Armed Services has contracts (including subcontracts) or grants (including subgrants) with the federal government, please provide the following information:

2017

Federal grant/ contract	Federal agency	Dollar value	Subject of contract or grant
None			

2016

Federal grant/ contract	Federal agency	Dollar value	Subject of contract or grant
None			

2015

Federal grant/ contract	Federal agency	Dollar value	Subject of contract or grant
None			

<u>Foreign Government Contract or Payment Information:</u> If you or the entity you represent before the Committee on Armed Services has contracts or payments originating from a foreign government, please provide the following information:

2017

Foreign contract/ payment	Foreign government	Dollar value	Subject of contract or payment
None			

2016

Foreign contract/ payment	Foreign government	Dollar value	Subject of contract or payment
None			

2015

Foreign contract/ payment	Foreign government	Dollar value	Subject of contract or payment
None